$\mathcal{W}$ORLDWIDE $\mathcal{A}$RCHAEOLOGY $\mathcal{S}$ERIES 14

THEORETICAL ROMAN ARCHAEOLOGY: SECOND CONFERENCE PROCEEDINGS

$\mathcal{W}$ORLDWIDE $\mathcal{A}$RCHAEOLOGY $\mathcal{S}$ERIES   SERIES EDITOR: ROSS SAMSON

edited by
PETER RUSH

THEORETICAL ROMAN ARCHAEOLOGY:
SECOND CONFERENCE PROCEEDINGS

Avebury
Aldershot · Brookfield USA · Hong Kong · Singapore · Sydney

CONTENTS

LIST OF CONTRIBUTORS

LINDSAY ALLASON-JONES	Archaeological Museums Officer, University and Society of Antiquaries of Newcastle upon Tyne Museum of Antiquities, University of Newcastle-upon-Tyne
SIMON CLARKE	Research Assistant, Department of Archaeological Sciences, University of Bradford
CAROL VAN DRIEL-MURRAY	Instituut voor Pre- en Protohistorische Archeologie, Universiteit van Amsterdam
SIMON P. ELLIS	Assistant Principal Planner, Lothian Regional Council
JEREMY EVANS	Free-lance Roman Pottery Consultant, Birmingham
IAIN FERRIS	Director, Birmingham University Field Archaeology Unit, University of Birmingham
MICHAEL J. JONES	Director of the City of Lincoln Archaeology Unit, Lincoln; Honorary Research Fellow of the University of Manchester
BERNICE KURCHIN	Research Student, Department of Anthropology, Hunter College, City University of New York
JASON MONAGHAN	Free-lance Archaeologist, St Peter Port, Guernsey
PETE RUSH	Research Assistant, Department of Archaeological Sciences, University of Bradford
ELEANOR SCOTT	Lecturer, King Alfred's College, Winchester

SARAH SCOTT   Research Fellow, Archaeology Depart-
                           ment, University of Durham

MANUELA STRUCK   Institut für Vor- und Frühgeschichte,
                           Johannes Gutenberg-Universitat, Mainz

TONY WILMOTT   English Heritage, Central Archaeology
                           Service, Fort Cumberland, Eastney

ACKNOWLEDGEMENTS

I would like to thank Simon Clarke, Rick Jones and Janice Rush who helped and gave advice during the editing of this volume. I would also like to thank all those who helped with the organising and running of TRAC 92 from which this book results. In particular Patrick Litherland and the Dept of Continuing Education at the University of Bradford; the chairs of the various sessions Lindsay Allason-Jones, Martin Millett, Jason Monaghan, Eleanor Scott, Tim Taylor and Tony Wilmott and also those who helped with registration and numerous other tasks and problems – Grace Ballance, Elizabeth Clark, Simon Doyle, Kath Evans, Seema Mann and Nuala Moran. I am also grateful to all those who attended the conference and to everyone who contributed a paper: Lindsay Allason-Jones, Simon Clarke, Carol van Driel-Murray, Simon P. Ellis, Jeremy Evans, Iain Ferris, Richard Hingley, Michael Jones, Rick Jones, Bernice Kurchin, Martin Millett, Jason Monaghan, Robert Rippengal, Eleanor Scott, Sarah Scott, Manuela Struck, Jeremy Taylor and Tony Wilmott.

INTRODUCTION

Pete Rush

Most of the papers contained within this volume are derived from papers that were originally given at the second Theoretical Roman Archaeology Conference (TRAC 92) held in the Department of Archaeology, University of Bradford on the 28th and 29th March 1992. In common with the first TRAC, held the year before at the University of Newcastle, no overall theme was imposed upon the conference with the aim of not limiting the topics discussed to any one narrow area. As a result the papers presented here cover a wide range of topics from questions of gender to finds research, from economics to burial practices, from urban geography to the interpretation of villa mosaics amongst others.

They are, however, linked by a central concern to challenge and re-examine the current traditional consensus that dominates Roman archae-ology. In this they also raise new questions and new areas of investigation some of which, most notably gender issues, have been ignored for too long and, as in the proceedings of the first TRAC (Scott 1993), they open the possibility of the development of a reinvigorated, critically self-aware and theoretically informed Roman archaeology. Below, I examine briefly some of the major themes that were brought out in many of the papers at the conference.

Lindsay Allason-Jones and Carol van Driel-Murray's chapters both reveal the effect that unexamined assumptions about the relationship of artefacts and gender have had upon interpretation. They provide important examples of how assumptions have become embedded within Roman archaeology and have taken on the appearance of fact. Allason-Jones argues that the interpretation of certain classes of artefact as associated with particular genders is a projection into the past of comtemporary views of such objects and suggests therefore that interpretations dependent on such data may need to be treated with circumspection. Van Driel-Murray avoids this problem by utilising data, in this case the evidence of Roman shoes, where gender may be inferred through sexual dimorphism. Her paper also shows the value of ethnographic and ethnohistorical parallels in understanding features of Roman society, an approach which has been uncommon in Roman archaeology.

Eleanor Scott in her paper presents a more radical critique of the androcentrism present within the subject. She provides a number of examples where women have been either excluded, marginalised, or represented in a distorted fashion in the texts of Roman archaeology, and she demonstrates the need for the critical examination of the basis of discipline.

Similarly, the chapters concerned with various facets of urbanism by Simon Clarke and Simon Ellis show the use of theoretical perspectives that are innovative within Roman archaeology and which break with the traditional pre-occupation with the constructional histories of towns and cities. Clarke applies central place theory to the location of small towns in Roman Britain and shows how a sophisticated version of this can help in understanding the nature of urban settlement. Ellis examines the internal structure of Roman urban sites through theories based in modern town planning and shows how these can elucidate the social and power effects of urban architecture.

Although, many of the papers at the conference and those included here argue for the wider adoption of explicitly theoretical viewpoints in Roman archaeology, either through direct argument or, implicitly, through example, there was an awareness that theory on its own is not enough. Both Jeremy Evans and Michael Jones, amongst others, voice this concern here. Evans argues that methodological care in the collection of data forms a necessary foundation to any interpretation whilst Jones is concerned that over indulgence in theoretical introspection will cause communication problems between different areas of Roman archaeology.

Taken together these papers show the possibilities that a variety of different theoretical perspectives offer for expanding the horizons of Roman archaeology. Hopefully, the papers of this volume, which continue on from the first TRAC volume, will be a catalyst for change within the subject. In common with the first conference the aim has not been to set a new agenda or to develop a new school of theoretical archaeology but to show the dangers of complacently continuing within the traditional framework without examining the possibility of doing Roman archaeology in other ways and of addressing new questions and areas of research.

That the need is felt acutely by some within the discipline is probably to be seen in the continued interest in participating in, attending, and holding more Theoretical Roman Archaeology Conferences (in Glasgow 1993, in Durham 1994, and Reading 1995, with more promised).

Reference

Scott, Eleanor (ed.) 1993. *Theoretical Roman Archaeology: First Conference Proceedings*. Avebury: Aldershot.

ridentem dicere verum quid vetat?
    – Horace (*Satires* I,1.24)

GENDER IN QUESTION[1]

Carol van Driel-Murray

At the first TRAC meeting, several of the contributors felt it necessary to stress their 'gender awareness', untrammelled by modern preconceptions – though the effect was somewhat marred by the ensuing unhesitating use of beads and bangles as indicators of female presence. Yet a glance at their own audience should have dispelled any illusions as to beads, bangles, long hair, or ear-rings being exclusive to females – in fact the converse was true. So, if in contemporary terms there is such a gap between the perceived and the apparent, how are we to fare with an ancient society where we know even less of the social conventions?

For the identification of women and children in archaeological contexts we must clearly turn to the external variables, as Binford's middle range theory exhorts us to do. Biological differences naturally lead to the cemeteries, but quite apart from the problems caused by cremation and small numbers, the trouble with burials is that the people contained were *dead* and don't tell us all that much about people in life: who was doing what, where, when, with whom, and how often. And if we are trying to establish the context of female existence, this is the information we need.

One biological variable that may be indirectly traceable in the detritus of a living population is body size. Since the female human tends in general to be smaller than the male, and this sexual dimorphism seems to be more marked in the ancient than the modern population (Wells 1982: 140), size

differences reflected in discarded clothing might be one way of approach-
ing the problem. Conveniently, virtually the only kind of Roman clothing
to survive intact – footwear – is also a relatively sensitive exponent of
sexual dimorphism. This allows us to exploit a number of very large
footwear complexes from a variety of Roman sites in north-western Europe
as a source of demographic information.

The foot is the first part of the human anatomy to reach adult dimen-
sions. After growing steadily throughout childhood, boys' and girls' sizes
begin to diverge from about the age of 10, with girls achieving their
full adult size between 11 and 13. Boys continue to grow till they reach
their larger, adult male sizes at about 15–16. The longer growth results in
a difference of about 2cm between the average foot size of adult females
and adult males. Naturally this is no absolute rule, but exceptions are only
a problem on the individual level, not in the context of the aggregate
groups which will be examined here. Slight differences between modern
statistics and those from the 19th century suggest that though the course of
growth is unchanged, children now are more advanced, so in antiquity the
divergence between girls and boys may have begun a little later and boys
may not all have reached their adult size till about 16–17. The size difference between males and females remains constant (Martin and Saller 1958:
971ff; Groenman-van Waateringe 1978; Grew and de Neergaard 1988:
103–105).

The normal size distribution of adult shoes illustrates both the differences between females and males (Fig. 1.1, 1–2) and the area of overlap
between the larger females and smaller males (Fig. 1.1, 3).[2] In archaeological footwear contexts, however, the groups are not neatly separated and
what we find is a continuum from the smallest babies' shoes (from 11cm)
to the largest male feet. Thus account has to be taken not only of the
overlap of females and males, but also of the growth of children into
adults, and in particular, the growth of boys into young men, since at this
time they occupy positions in the normal female range. In reality, this is
proportionally not a major source of error since boys' shoes in the range
35–40 only account for about 5% of the total (van den Burg 1948: 39[2]),
though on an individual level this remains the most problematical category.
If the modern distribution is translated into archaeological terms, a normal
population would appear as Figure 1.1, 4, with the female range of sizes
exaggerated by a) growing youths and b) overlap with the tail end of the
male distribution.

That this is indeed the pattern found in most large medieval urban com

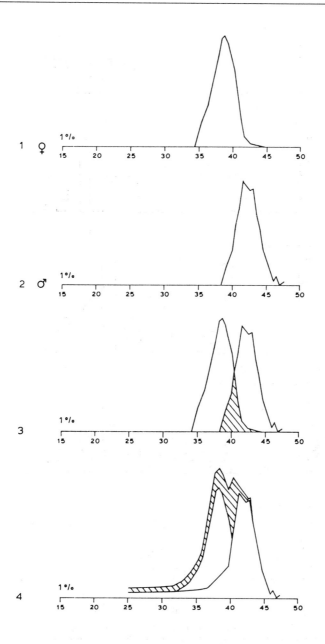

Figure 1.1. Modern shoe sizes (after Groenman-van Waateringe 1978: fig. 2).
1. women, 2. men, 3. combined showing overlap, 4. as found.

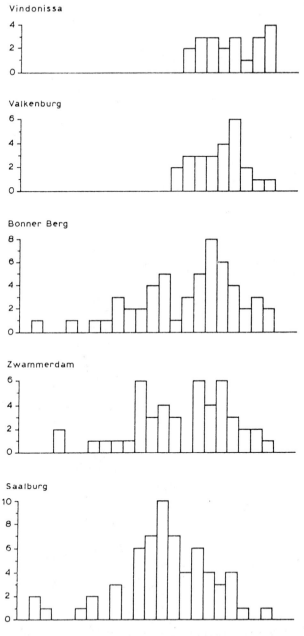

Figure 1.2. Size distributions from Roman sites (relative scale).

plexes (Groenman-van Waateringe 1978; Grew and de Neergaard 1988: 104) as well as on Roman sites (Fig. 1.2, Saalburg, Zwammerdam) suggests that foot size as reflected by footwear is a valid criterion for distinguishing men, women and children as components of a living population. Though children's shoes can to some extent be correlated to age, there is no differentiation beyond these three categories. At this point it may justifiably be questioned whether such an obvious finding could even be relevant. However, in the context of Roman military sites, the proportions between the categories do become interesting because it is generally accepted that there was a legal ban on the marriage of soldiers (Campbell 1978; Saller and Shaw 1984: 143–44). Even by contemporaries this ban was regarded as an extra hardship to be endured and the awkward legal consequences were mitigated by successive emperors until the restriction was eventually lifted by Septimius Severus at the end of the second century. When an authority as eminent as Calvin Wells invokes the unmarried veterans, still dependent on the 'pleasant' (though apparently restricted) amenities of Cirencester's prostitutes to explain the imbalance in sex-ratio in a cemetery founded over *one century* after this ban had been lifted (Wells 1982: 135), one realises just how deeply this typically 19th century notion of segregated military communities pervades thought on Roman military life and, indeed, the entire subject of interaction between soldiers and civilians.

Looking at the distribution of shoe sizes from the first century military sites (Fig. 1.2: Valkenburg, Vindonissa) we find, not a normal population, but a single curve, corresponding to the modern graph (Fig. 1.1, 2) for adult males.[3] Thus the expectations of unmarried soldiers, living in a closed camp are fulfilled. Though the analysis is not yet complete, the footwear from the early first century fort at Velsen shows a similar pattern. In all three cases, the footwear represents the population of the camp interior (van Driel-Murray 1985: 49–53) and the possibility of camp villages outside is therefore not excluded. These forts date to the unstable, campaigning phase of Roman expansion, when family life would indeed be difficult to maintain.

In the second century, however, the picture changes (Fig. 1.2: Saalburg, Zwammerdam). The graphs for the mixed *vicus* and fort refuse dumps at Zwammerdam and the Saalburg reveal relatively balanced populations with large numbers of children and only a slight preponderance of males, in no way resembling the male dominated communities envisaged by Wells, Saller and Shaw or others. As might have been expected, permanent forts, surrounded by permanent *vici* were evidently more conducive to family life.

VINDOLANDA: A CASE STUDY ————

The site of Vindolanda on Hadrian's Wall (Birley 1977 and in press) provides considerable refinement due to the large amount of footwear distributed over four well-dated phases (periods I-IV) between c. AD 90–120
and the availability of two control groups from the later ditches. In addition, written documents give a unique insight into the individuals and the
units occupying the earlier phases, thus providing an interpretative framework for the analysis of finds from the site. The finds from the earlier
phases come from demolition levels which seal rubbish left by the previous
occupants. Here, as at Valkenburg (van Driel-Murray 1985: 49–53) old
buildings were flattened and refuse was levelled off to raise the level of the
wet and subsiding site for the next building phase. Concentrations of particular kinds of refuse indicate that find distribution does actually reflect the
activities being carried out in the buildings in the final period of their
occupation and is not refuse brought in for the purpose of levelling. Period
V is excluded as it is an ill-defined secondary deposit.

The distribution of shoe sizes from the two ditches (Fig. 1.4, top two
graphs) is pretty well identical to that from the Saalburg and Zwammerdam, which are comparable in context and date, with the expected over-
representation of female sizes characteristic of a normal balanced population. Incidentally, in medieval contexts, the number of children's shoes
forms an index of generally rising living standards: if this criterion is applicable to Roman times, then the *vici* of Vindolanda seem to have been relatively prosperous.

The quantity of footwear from period I is insufficient for conclusions to
be warranted, but by period II numbers have increased. The footwear
comes from deposits covering the *praetorium*, the quarters of the com-
manding officer and his staff, in this case either Vettius Severus or Flavius
Genialis, prefects of the Cohors VIIII Batavorum (Birley 1990: 18 and in
press). The distribution is much as Valkenburg, mainly male sizes at 34 and
above. Making allowances for the tailing off of male sizes, this probably
leaves one woman (or youth) and a child for the prefect's household, a not
unexpected picture. One of the prefects possessed a natty pair of openwork shoes in size 39 (Fig. 1.5).

Period III ended in AD 103. Preparations for departure appear to have
been quite hurried and a lot of material was abandoned more or less in
situ. Concentrations of characteristic debris suggest that tents were being
checked and recycled in the *praetorium* courtyard and horse gear, including

chamfrons, was being refurbished in one of the side rooms. The *praetorium* may, therefore have functioned as a collection and sorting point in the last weeks of occupation in addition to being the residence of the commander. The footwear shows a different pattern to the other earlier military sites, due to the presence of a number of distinct individuals, each represented by several shoes sometimes in pairs and often of different styles (Fig. 1.3, period III; Fig. 1.7). Despite the disapprobation of the rigidly theoretical, the abundant documentation makes it tempting to link these distinctive feet to the inhabitants of the *praetorium*. Flavius Cerialis, the commander, with exceptionally elaborate openwork shoes (which for full effect must have been worn with coloured socks); his wife, Sulpicia Lepidina with a narrow, extremely elegant foot, size 33 (Fig. 1.3, individual 6; Fig. 1.7, no. 862). She had sensible closed shoes as well as fashionable sandals stamped with the maker's name: Lucius Aebutius Thales, surely the first designer label in history (Fig. 1.6). Her foot shape is virtually unique, of all the hundreds of soles from the site, only one resembles it. This is a smaller version (Fig. 1.3, individual 5b with shoes and sandals; Fig. 1.7, no. 313 and 1541) and from the same level: a daughter or a servant? There is a whole group of children, four of the shoes possibly from the same individual growing from a baby to a child of 5/6 (Fig. 1.3, individuals 1–4; Fig. 1.7 nos 398, 431), then an older boy (Fig. 1.3, individual 5a; Fig. 1.7 no. 1520) with expensive openwork shoes who oddly and characteristically scuffed the out-side of his left foot. Are these the 'pueros tuos' of the letter Inv. 412? (Birley in press; van Driel-Murray, in press). This is an exceptional case of individuals identifiable through a combination of circumstances and the conclusions are unlikely to be generally applicable. Apart from these indi-viduals and a few isolated soles in the range 27–34 which may belong to the household, the pattern is the expected male, military model.

On withdrawal of the Batavian cohort, the structures of period III were demolished, covered with turf and a barrack block was erected on the site in AD 104 (dendro date; Birley in press). The garrison now seems to have been the Cohors I Tungrorum, with evidence for legionary detachments appearing in some of the texts. The actual room deposits of course reflect the final occupation and probably date to c. 115/120 after which the whole site was cleared for the *fabrica* of period V. Gone are the individuals of period III: a few pairs can be identified, but there are only three possible 'individuals'. The majority of soles are large, with 34 still marking the bottom end of the male range. But in addition, there are a fair number of women and children here, actually inside the barrack block (Fig. 1.3,

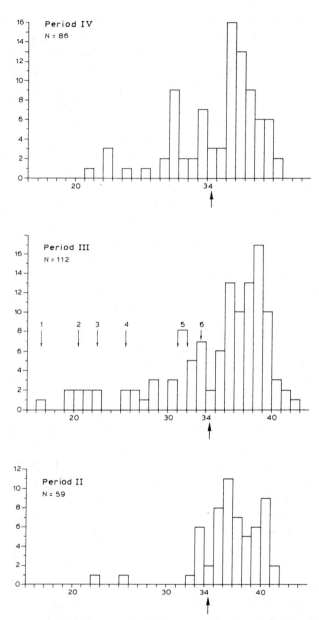

Figure 1.3. Vindolanda shoe sizes by period. Arrow points to male/female overlap, numerals in period III indicate discrete individuals. (Period II c. AD 90–95; period III c. 95–102/3; period IV 104 – c. 120.)

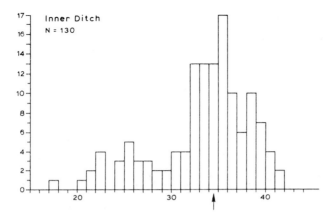

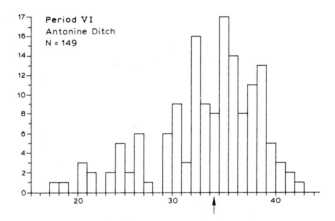

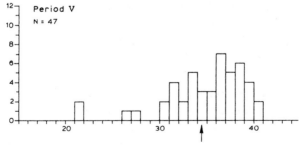

Figure 1.4. Vindolanda shoe sizes by period. Arrow points to male/female overlap. (Period V c. 120 – mid-2nd cent.; period VI late 2nd cent.; Inner Ditch 3rd cent.)

period IV; Fig. 1.9).

While we may have been prepared for some form of family life in the settlements outside the forts, cohabitation inside the fort at this date is unexpected, to say the least.

The unconscious model for Roman camp organisation has always been drawn from British military practice with garrisons regarded as military preserves, occupied with noble and dedicated young men, strictly segregated from the surrounding settlements. Brothels under military supervision cater for physical needs and that is the limit of 'native interaction'. This view lies behind the bleak and loveless picture of military life accepted by Wells (1982), Saller and Shaw (1984: 142) and Gilliam (1978; quoted in Roxan 1991: 465). But the Dutch military authorities tended to be more pragmatic and they also tolerated a far greater degree of mixing between Europeans and natives. To me the situation in the Vindolanda barrack is recognisable as the archaeological exponent of the system of camp concubinage, as practised by the Dutch forces stationed in the Indonesian colonies in the recent past. Without going into too many details here, it may be profitable to look at the workings of this system as an alternative form of military organisation in which unofficial unions were officially tolerated (de Braconier 1913; van der Wurff-Bodt 1989).

Until well into the 20th century, common soldiers in Dutch military service were not permitted to marry at all, while officers had to meet exorbitant property qualifications before an application for marriage would even be considered. The reasons were unashamedly financial. Pay for the lower ranks was poor and it was readily admitted that if soldiers were to be allowed to marry, wages would have to be substantially increased. The military authorities were reluctant to bear the costs of providing transport and accommodation for families, and above all, the cost of the widow's pension, to which officially married couples were entitled. Essentially, these are the reasons for the Roman ban, but then clothed in finer sounding terms (Campbell 1978: 154).

Despite the official ban, and with full connivance of the authorities, European[4] soldiers in Indonesia did have wives: concubines taken from the native population associated with the camp (in Roman terms, the *vicus*). This population (the *vicani*) came to constitute almost a separate cast, having little contact with the surrounding native population, though in some cases still linked to it through ties of kin. With their disregard for constraining native traditions, their military orientation, and their language laced with pidgin terms, these villagers were totally dependent on the army

Figure 1.5. Openwork shoe, Vindolanda period II.

presence and could, like their Roman equivalents, hardly be termed 'civilian' in the conventional sense. As late as 1905, when marriage conditions for officers had been considerably eased, half of the officers and c. 16% of the common soldiers, most of those serving more than the standard 6-year term, still had a native concubine or 'housekeeper'. The native Indonesian forces, which made up 2/3 of army strength, were almost all married under their own, Islamic, law, but as this was not recognised, these women were also regarded as concubines by the military authorities. Not that it made any difference to their rights under local law as regards dowry, inheritance or property. The women had to be registered by the camp authorities as official concubines, with a ration entitlement and with specific rights and duties. Until the early years of the 20th century only the officers had separate accommodation: the rest, married and single alike, slept in the communal dormitories. Children slept in either a hammock slung above the bed or on the floor under it, the meagre possessions stored in a chest or on a shelf running the length of the barrack block. To modern sensibilities, the lack of privacy is astonishing, but conditions in native *kampongs* and, indeed, the wretched homes from which most European recruits were drawn were hardly better. With moral pressure growing in the Netherlands towards the end of the 19th century, the military authorities became remarkably active in defense of the system of camp concubinage. Novels appeared describing the life of concubines and the issue was discussed in leading liberal magazines (Si-Tamoe-Lama, 1913; de Braconier, 1913). The military authorities had little time for moral arguments about the holy state of matrimony: they recognised concubinage

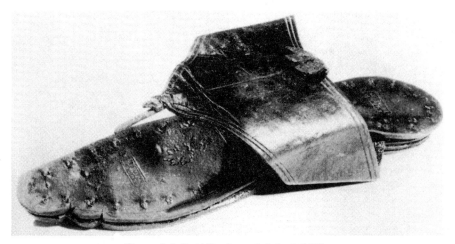

Figure 1.6. Lepidina's sandal, period III.

as one of the few mitigating features in the comfortless, ill paid life of the soldiers. It was seen as a stabilising factor, reducing crime and especially drunkenness, encouraging men to sign up for a further 6 year term of duty. Maintaining a concubine encouraged thrift – indeed, wages and rations were paid direct to her.[5] Criticism was countered by placing curtains between the beds in dormitories and allowing more space for co-habiting men.

The women left the barracks in the morning, spending the day in a specially built women's hall washing, cooking and doing odd jobs to earn money. Concubinage may have been advantageous for men and authorities, but for the women it was simply a case of survival. If a soldier died or was killed on duty, she had no rights and she and her children were turned out immediately, their only hope being to find someone else to take them on. As most men eventually returned to Europe, abandonment was almost inevitable and women attempted to make some provision for the eventuality. The lack of provision for women in soldiers' wills, noted by Roxan (1991: 465) is perhaps suggestive of similar relationships, though the strength of local customary law should not be underestimated. Despite the uncertainties potential concubines seem to have preferred European soldiers (they earned more). A form of upward mobility: one wonders whether the legionary detachments at Vindolanda had the same advantage over the Tungrian auxiliaries.

The real problem was formed by the children. Boys were expected to

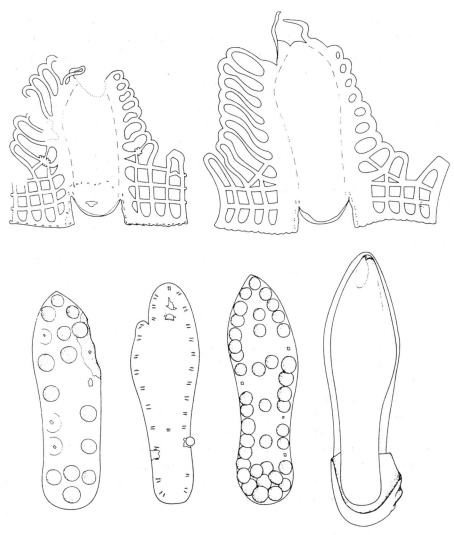

*Figure 1.7. Selection of period III individuals (scale c. 2:7): individual 2,
431; individual 4, 398; individual 5a, 1520; individual 5b, 313, 1541;
individual 6, 862.*

join the native forces, as their Roman counterparts did, but for girls there
was little hope other than concubinage or prostitution: 'it is a melancholy
fact that many, if not most, daughters of the European common soldiers
are, in a sense, *compelled* to prostitute themselves, as they are destitute of
any provision' (Ducimus 1902: 196, original emphasis). If the same applied

to the Roman *vicus* inhabitants, we may have one more reason why so few daughters appear on diplomas (Roxan 1991: 465–66). Despite the glory, fine uniforms and regular, if low, pay, the soldiers and the camp population were despised by both the native Indonesians and the Europeans of the administrative levels: mixed race children were unacceptable to either group. Thus between the native population and the governing elite was a third element, the military population with its own culture, its own symbolism of status, centred on itself and essentially self-perpetuating. With the lack of evidence for Roman interaction on native settlements in northern Britain, this perhaps encapsulates the social isolation of the forts along Hadrian's Wall. Enclave theory seems more promising than frontier theory in this situation.

The size distribution of the footwear from Vindolanda period IV fulfills all expectations of camp concubinage. There are further implications: the women spend most of the day outside the fort (in one of the *vicus* buildings of uncertain function?[6]) so most female activities and their attendant losses of personal ornaments and tools will also be found outside. Indonesian women returned to their families or to a female relative with a home in the camp village to give birth to their children, so we would not even expect to find dead new-borns under barrack floors as proof of female presence. These women would have been largely invisible in the material culture of the fort itself.

Even by ancient standards, it might be awkward to accommodate men, wives and children in the familiar bunks of the 8 man *contubernium,* so if concubinage were a regular practice there were evidently fewer men to a barrack block than usually envisaged at this date. It is perhaps unlikely that all men would have a concubine and it may be that only one or two rooms were set aside for such men. The distribution of footwear belonging to women and children in the Vindolanda barrack is suggestive of this (Fig. 1.8).

The other small finds from the barrack block are scrappy and rather sparse, the sort of oddments people would discard when sorting out their possessions.[7] Demolition and levelling in preparation for the next construction phase has tended to spread material, so find distribution need not exactly represent actual room activity, but that it does bear some resemblance is suggested by the spread of soles fitting together, forming a pair or clearly belonging to the same individual. The quite marked concentration of women's and children's shoes in rooms III and IV (Fig. 1.8) suggests these may be the 'married quarters'. Although the officers' quarters at the end have been only partially excavated, there is a curious absence of female footwear here.

Sewing needles, broken knives, bronze *spatulae* and bone or glass gaming counters are appropriate soldierly attributes, along with a single *lorica* plate, a loop junction and quite a number of bolt heads. Considering the obvious literacy of the soldiers, the number of *styli* (8) is hardly unexpected. The only remotely female items – in a conventional sense – are a pin, a ring, a penannular brooch, two long hair pins and a fair number of wooden combs. None of this is especially conclusive: I presume that men also occasionally combed their hair. Other than their shoes, the women and children have left remarkably little trace of their presence. What is interesting is the amount of broken furniture – chair legs and boxes – which hints at some standard of comfort and perhaps also at rather more space in rooms than if 8 men lived in each. Also notable amongst the finds are the number of broken wooden barrels: for food storage and interior toilets perhaps? There appears to have been a toilet pit in room XV, so sanitary arrangements for ladies seem to have been catered for. It seems unlikely that the conventional 80 man unit was squeezed into this particular barrack block.

The Indonesian concubines considered themselves to be properly married and they were regarded as respectable members of camp society. It is clear that there was a widespread aspiration to the formation of stable, nuclear relationships (*contubernium*) between men and women who were, for a variety of reasons excluded from full Roman citizen marriage in its strictly legalistic interpretation (Rawson 1974; Treggiari 1981). *Contubernium* applied to a range of such conditions, including what was probably full marriage under native law and custom and would be equally appropriate to the status of Indonesian camp concubines, even down to the multiple *contubernia* (Treggiari 1981: 61). That the word also applied to the soldier's messmates perhaps helped to obscure *de facto* marriages in camp records. It is surely no coincidence that a document from the period IV barrack itself should refer to the *contibernalis* (sic) of Tagamatos the standard bearer (Birley 1990: 29–30, T944). If this person was female, she clearly controlled finances in much the same way as the fictitious Saridjem (Si-Tamoe-Lama 1913).

The evidence from period IV for women and children may not seem very strong, but it does not stand alone. Exactly contemporary is the legionary *fabrica* on the Bonner Berg (van Driel-Murray and Gechter 1983). The footwear distribution is remarkably similar to that of Vindolanda period IV

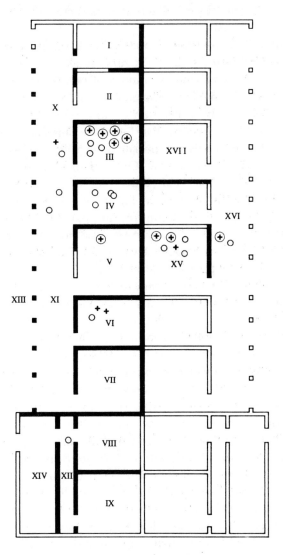

+ children < 19 cm

⊕ w / c 19 / 20 cm

O women 20.5 - 22.5 cm

Figure 1.8. Vindolanda period IV barrack (restored), location of smaller soles: children <19cm (to size 38); juvenile/small adult 19–20 cm (28–30); small adult 20–22.5 cm (30–34).

(compare Fig. 1.2. with Fig. 1.3). Writing in 1980, and faced with what seemed to be an impossible situation, I made ridiculous attempts to explain away the small sizes as very young recruits (op. cit.: 23). They must have been amazingly young to still be in the juvenile stages of growth evidenced by 20 individuals below size 34, which, as at Vindolanda, marks the tail end of the adult male distribution. Thus are we blinded by our preconceptions: it is now perfectly obvious that these are the concubines and children of legionaries, helping their menfolk out with tasks outside the camp, just as their Indonesian counterparts were to do 1700 years later.

GENDER IN QUESTION ——————

Though with its relatively low-key involvement and its tolerance of native systems, the Dutch colonial experience may be a more useful source of enlightenment than the British, a more serious criticism which may be levelled against the present construct is that it is patently founded on personal preconceptions. Here, I have assumed that men and women aspire to permanent unions. But this is the question posed in the title. *I* consciously prefer to see women and children living in concubinage in the barrack, but with a different life-style I might be tempted in another direction.

It has already been mentioned that the female size distribution is distorted by the presence of boys growing through these sizes to reach their ultimate adult size. It is, therefore, possible that all sizes below 34 (the standard tail end of adult males throughout all Vindolanda periods) belong to boys and juveniles (Figs 1.3 and 1.4). Because it is not a consistent curve, but bi-modal, like that at Bonn (Fig. 1.2), some of the older, but still growing boys are absent. In other words, we would be left with the beardless youths so beloved of Latin poets: the predilections of Julius Caesar and, indeed, Hadrian himself need no further elaboration. Under this model, the concentration in rooms III and IV look, I am sorry to say, more like a male brothel than anything else. I am culturally adverse to the idea of children abused in the barracks at Vindolanda, but given a different society, and especially a slave society, it might not have been seen that way. As yet it is impossible to separate male and female footwear except for a few highly distinctive and fashionable styles. Lepidina's 'daughter' had a very serviceable pair of boots masking the extreme elegance of the sole and the foot impression within. So we come to a full circle again. The impossibility of indisputably defining female presence leaves two alternatives to choose from. Both have repercussions on the population density in the camps and raise questions as to the actual strength of the garrisons. Both improve the lot of the hapless soldier in bleak frontier garrisons.

NOTES ————

1. The contribution presented at TRAC 2 and printed here is a preliminary version of a paper due to be more fully expanded elsewhere.

2. British children's sizes 1–13, adults 1–12; continental sizes are foot length in cm x 1.5.

3. Figures from production of footwear for issue on ration in the Netherlands in 1947, hence not affected by the vagaries of consumer choice.

4. I use 'European' since only about 50% actually came from the Netherlands. The rest was composed of Germans, Belgians and Danes – about as ethnically mixed as the Roman forces.

5. Prostitution and the attendant VD infections were seen as a far greater threat to the morals of the force: comparisons unfavourable to the British practices were drawn. There, the military brothels, medically controlled or not, resulted in an annual VD infection of 45%, as against 35% for the Dutch forces, concentrated mainly in the single term group, and only 18% amongst the native forces, who were almost all married (Ducimus 1902: 189).

6. Building XI for example, which lies just outside the military annex of the 'Vicus' I might be a later candidate.

7. For the find distribution I am indebted to R. Birley, who made the lists available to me prior to publication (Birley in press).

Bibliography

Birley, R. 1977. *Vindolanda, a Roman Frontier Post on Hadrian's Wall.* London.

Birley, R. 1990. *The Roman Documents from Vindolanda.* Greenhead.

Birley, R. n.d. *Vindolanda Guide.* Greenhead.

Birley, R. in press. *The Early Timber Forts at Vindolanda.*

de Braconier, A. 1913. Het kazerne-concubinaat in Nederlandsch Indië, *Vragen van den Dag* 28:974–995.

van den Burg, G. 1948. *Handboek voor den schoenhandel 1948.* Nijmegen.

Campbell, B. 1978. The Marriage of Soldiers under the Empire. *Journal of Roman Studies* 68:153–166.

van Driel-Murray, Carol 1985. The Production and Supply of Military Leather Work in the First and Second Centuries A.D.: a Review of the Archaeological Evidence. In M. C. Bishop (ed.), *The Production and Distribution of Roman Military Equipment*, 43–81. Oxford, British Archaeological Reports (Int. Ser. 275).

van Driel-Murray, Carol in press. The Footwear. In Birley.

van Driel-Murray, Carol and M. Gechter 1983. Funde aus der fabrica der legio I Minervia im Bonner Berg. *Rheinische Ausgrabungen* 23, *Beiträge zur Archäologie des römische Rheinlands* 4:1–83.

'Ducimus' 1901. Het kazerne-concubinaat. *Indisch Militair Tijdschrift* 32:643–659.

'Ducimus' 1902. Het prostitutie vraagstuk in het Indische leger. *Indisch Militair Tijdschrift* 33:188–212.

Grew, F. and M. de Neergaard, 1988. Shoes and Patterns. *Medieval Finds from Excavations in London* 2, London.

Groenman-van Waateringe, W. 1978. Shoe Sizes and Paleodemography? *Helinium* 18:184–189.

Martin R. and K. Saller 1958. *Lehrbuch der Anthropologie.* 3rd ed. Stuttgart.

Rawson, B. 1974. Roman Concubinage and Other *De Facto* Marriages. *Transactions of the American Philological Association* 104:279–305.

Roxan, M. M. 1991. Women on the Frontiers. In V. A. Maxfield and M. J. Dobson (eds), *Roman Frontier Studies 1989,* 462–467. (Proceedings of the XVth International Congress of Roman Frontier Studies, Exeter 1991).

Saller, R. P. and B. D. Shaw, 1984. Tombstones and Roman Family Relationships in the Principate: Civilians, Soldiers and Slaves. *Journal of Roman Studies* 74:124–156.

Si-Tamoe-Lama, 1913. *Saridjem – de kazerne huishoudster.* Utrecht.

Treggiari, S. 1981. *Contubernales* in CIL 6. *Phoenix* 35:42–69.

Wells, C. 1982. The Human Burials. In A. McWhirr, L. Viner and C. Wells (eds), *Romano-British Cemeteries at Cirencester,* 135–202. (Cirencester Excavations II, Cirencester 1982).

van der Wurf-Bodt, C. 1989. Het kazerneconcubinaat in Indie. *Spiegel Historiael* 24:222–226.

2

'Sexing' Small Finds

Lindsay Allason-Jones

John Clayton in 1880, when discussing why Coventina's Well was full of artefacts, put forward the hypothesis that 'lovesick damsels cast into the Well their spare trinkets in the hope of obtaining the countenance of the Goddess in their views'. 'To these interesting ladies we are doubtless indebted for the brooches, rings, and beads found in the Well' (Clayton 1880: 31). In 1979 Charles Daniels wrote of the buildings, referred to as 'chalets', discovered during his excavations at Housesteads: 'both Mr Gillam and the writer were struck by the preponderance of brooches and other trinkets at Housesteads XIII. To the writer this suggested that the chalets had been married quarters of some sort' (Daniels 1980: 189). Both archaeologists, separated by one hundred years of improved archaeological techniques, were basing their hypotheses on the premise that there were certain small finds which could be identified as having been used or worn by men and others only by women. With the recent development of interest in the topic of gender in archaeology many researchers are being tempted to base their theories of space allocation/role/status, etc., on the evidence of small finds. This paper looks at some groups of finds from Romano-British contexts, traditionally regarded as 'female', in order to see if there really are classes of artefact which might be assigned to gender – might be termed 'male' or 'female'.

Many archaeologists have continued to follow Clayton and Daniels' view that brooches are indicative of a female presence despite the overwhelming evidence for men wearing brooches throughout the period of Roman Britain. Almost every military and civilian tombstone where the deceased is shown wearing a cloak has a brooch clearly visible fastening the garment (see for example: Ribchester: Shotter 1973a: pl.16; Housesteads: Coulston and Phillips 1988: nos 202–203; Vindolanda: ibid. no. 212). Philpott, in his extremely useful survey, *Burial Practices in Roman Britain*, has pointed out that 'sexual determinations of cemeteries have shown that males are often provided with a brooch at a number of sites, while the evidence of sexed late Iron Age cremations from King Harry Lane indicates that brooches were buried equally often with males and females . . . . The provision of brooches with males in cremations is mirrored in the mid-late 1st century in Dorset and Wessex, where brooches were largely confined to males and children in native inhumations' (1991: 123).

Having clarified the point that both men and women wore brooches is it possible to discover whether certain types of brooches were worn only by women while other types were confined to male costume? Theoretically one should be able to use the evidence from the cemeteries with this precision. Unfortunately, few cemetery reports are detailed enough. Even when the sex of the skeleton is given in association with a list of grave goods many of the older reports record merely 'a fibula' with no indication as to type.

One of the few cemetery reports which might be used to attribute gender to a brooch type is the Lankhills report (Clarke 1979) as only the male graves contained brooches, all of which were the 3rd – 4th century massive crossbow type, which have occasionally been described as insignia of rank for military or civilian officials. On the continent, however, such brooches have been found in female graves and it is possible that the gold example from The Wincle, Cheshire, found with necklaces and ear-rings, may be from a female grave (Johns, Thompson and Wagstaffe 1981).

Is it possible to make a judgement on the reasons why brooches were worn? Brooches would have been an essential feature of some Romano-British women's wardrobe as a few ensembles were literally pinned together. The costume now named after a woman called Menimane from Mainz-Weisenau (Espérandieu 1922: no. 5815) is the most obvious example. This was worn in the northern provinces in the pre-Roman Iron Age and the Roman period up to the early 2nd century AD, reappearing briefly in the 5th century. Menimane's costume included a closely fitting bodice fastened at the front by a brooch; over this she wore a loose tubular tunic, pinned at the shoulders by a pair of brooches with a third at the breast. Women wearing a similar outfit would have needed at least three brooches and many preferred more (see Wild 1968: fig. 21).

Women from the area of the Danube wore overtunics caught by a pair of brooches which were linked across the chest by a chain (Wild 1968: 207); so is it possible to attribute matching pairs of brooches to women, particularly those chained together? As men would have only needed a single brooch to fasten a cloak one might conclude that pairs of brooches linked by a thread or a chain were worn exclusively by women, although the evidence is not irrefutable. If the hypothesis does hold good then can one presume that any brooch which has been seen as one of a pair can be claimed as a female type? Unfortunately this is unlikely. Headstud brooches, trumpet brooches, disc brooches, and innumerable other types are found with chains or with the loops for attaching chains. The headloop is a feature which is rarely found on the Continent, despite the evidence for linked brooches on the Danubian tombstones, but it is a common element in the 1st and 2nd century British brooches and is ubiquitous on the trumpets, headstuds and other bow brooches which some specialists in the past have described as 'military'.

It is also possible to overemphasise the need for women to wear brooches to fasten their clothing. Not all women in Britain wore Menimane's costume or Danubian dress, the majority apparently preferring the Gallic coat worn by men, women and children throughout the Roman period. As this was a T-shaped roomy garment with a slit neck it required no brooches to hold it in position (Wild 1968: fig. 1). Wild has stated that clothing which needed more than one brooch to fasten it was rare in the north and that which needed a linked pair of brooches was confined to women who followed Continental styles of dressing.

As brooches continued to be manufactured and worn when Menimane's costume was out of fashion it must be presumed that some people wore brooches purely for decorative rather than functional purposes. The small triskele brooches and enamelled animal brooches are too small to fasten bulky woollen cloth and could be described as decorative only, but other types could be used for either purpose. Clearly more work is required in this area but the results so far seem to indicate that brooches were sexless; that they were bought by men and women alike, according to personal taste. If a man wanted to wear a small openwork triskele he did so, and if a woman wanted to wear a large crossbow brooch there was little to stop her. Loops were provided in case the purchaser needed to wear the brooches in a pair or attach a safety chain.

If it is difficult to determine whether a particular type of brooch was worn by men or women is it any easier with other types of jewellery?

Among the inhabitants of the city of Rome the wearing of ear-rings was purely for decorative purposes and strictly confined to women. To their historians and geographers the idea of men wearing ear-rings was simply evidence of the barbarity of foreigners and worthy of outraged comment. Isodorus (*Orig.* XIX.31.10) mentions that it was the fashion for Greek youths to wear a single ear-ring in one ear. Pliny (*Nat. Hist.* XI.50) was horrified that 'in the East, indeed, it is considered becoming even for men to wear gold in that place' (i.e. in the ear lobe). Other authors felt it was worthwhile to mention foreign men wearing ear-rings: Xenophon (*Anab.* III.1.31) refers to the Lydians; Juvenal (1.104) to the Babylonians; Macrobinus (*Sat.* VII.3) to the Libyans; and Plautus (*Poen.* V.2.21) to the Carthaginians.

If one looks at the coinage of the eastern kings, such as Phraates and Bahram, however, it is noticeable that they all wear ear-rings, from Phraates in 3 BC to Yazdgard in AD 457 (Toynbee 1978). In fact, throughout the period of the Roman empire the male rulers of the east and their subjects wore ear-rings and may have regarded them as a sign of rank.

The Roman army included many men from the eastern provinces and Africa where it was not considered improper or unusual for men to wear ear-rings. Despite the classical authors' disapproval of the practice it is possible that some of these troops continued to wear ear-rings during their military service in Britain. Unfortunately, there are no literary references which state categorically whether a serving auxiliary was or was not allowed to wear ear-rings. No ear-rings have been found in an indisputable relationship with a male skeleton in a Romano-British context, although bearing in mind the earlier remarks about brooches in cemeteries this is hardly surprising. Lankhills cemetery, which might have been of assistance, produced no ear-rings at all, even in the female graves (Clarke 1979), while the northern military cemeteries, such as Petty Knowes (Charlton and Day 1984), have produced very few metal artefacts other than coffin nails, hobnails and coins for Charon's fee. Ear-rings are not depicted on military tombstones but neither do they appear on the tombstones of women – the only exception being Regina from South Shields, who is depicted in the Palmyrene tradition and invariably is the exception to every rule (*CSIR* I.1. no. 147).

On the other hand, a large number of ear-rings come from forts and fortresses. Unfortunately, few come from firm contexts and many may have come from the *vici* or other areas where the presence of women would not have been unusual. A few, however, come from what might be seen as good military contexts. For example, two penannular copper alloy ear-rings come from Longthorpe (Frere and St. Joseph 1974: 62 fig. 32 no. 78; Allason-Jones 1989a: nos. 317 and 318). This fortress was occupied from c. AD 44/8 to c. AD 62, an early period for women to be present in any numbers. One ear-ring was found in the *praetentura* whilst the other was found in building X, which Frere and St. Joseph suggested might be an auxiliary *praetorium*. This last example was found in association with an armlet and a nail cleaner and might suggest the presence of an officer's wife or daughter – the Vindolanda writing tablets have shown that some officers were accompanied by their families at a very early stage despite official disapproval (Bowman and Thomas 1986: 122; Tacitus *Annals* III.33). An armlet and a nail cleaner are not very convincing evidence for the presence of women either, as will be discussed later.

The majority of forts which have produced ear-rings are in the area of Hadrian's Wall, although none of the milecastles or turrets of that frontier have produced examples (Allason-Jones 1988). All three units raised in areas known to have favoured ear-rings, which are attested in Britain, were stationed in the north: the Hamian archers from Syria at Carvoran and Bar Hill, the *numerus Maurorum Aurelianorum* at Burgh-by-Sands, and the Tigris Bargemen from Mesopotamia at South Shields and possibly Lancaster (Breeze and Dobson 1978; but see Shotter 1973b for the latter). Of these only South Shields has produced any ear-rings (Allason-Jones 1989a: nos. 480–88) but equally only South Shields could be regarded as having been extensively excavated. The evidence for eastern or African troops in Britain wearing ear-rings is, therefore, slight but should not be disregarded. The literary sources are silent on whether the men of Gaul or the Germanies or even Iron Age Britain wore ear-rings but it would be rash to take this as firm evidence that it was not done. It is only possible to say that in Britain some foreign troops or merchants may have continued their native tradition of wearing ear-rings as they continued to prefer their native costume. After all, if the Syrian archers did not give up wearing their flowing robes when they were sent on foreign postings it is unlikely that they gave up their ear-rings.

Solid neck-rings or torcs were worn as symbols of power and status in pre-Roman Britain and as such had magico-religious significance. Dio Cassius (LXII.2.4) tells us that Boudica wore 'a great twisted gold necklace' when she led the Iceni into battle, indicating that she had taken on the authority of a Celtic warrior chieftain symbolically. During the Roman period torcs were awarded to soldiers for acts of bravery but later came to be regarded merely as good luck symbols (Maxfield 1974) and were frequently worn as such by women (e.g. Regina *CSIR* I.i. no. 247). Necklaces made from beads seem to have been worn by women purely for decorative purposes (see Volusia Faustina: Allason-Jones 1989b: pl.23) but they were also worn by children of both sexes to support amulets. Melon beads of blue glass are usually found individually and one discovered attached to a *dolabra* sheath in Bonn Museum indicates that they too had an amuletic significance and may have been worn around the necks of either sex on leather thongs or copper alloy wire. In Rome itself the practice of men wearing necklaces and bracelets was considered to be on a par with wearing ear-rings: Diodorus Siculus (V.45) was disparaging about the Panchaeans who wore 'ornaments of gold, not only the women but the men as well, with collars of twisted gold about their necks, bracelets on their wrists, and rings hanging from their ears, after the manner of the Persians'. Clearly the arguments rehearsed previously about men of eastern origin wearing ear-rings can be extended to necklaces and bracelets, both of which can be seen on male Romano-Egyptian mummy portraits from the Fayum (Bowman 1990: pl. 9). There is evidence for gold armlets being male accessories in the early Celtic world (Strabo IV.4.5), and the massive armlets found in Iron Age contexts may well be a reflection of the use of torcs as symbols of the warrior class (see Anderson 1904). Unlike ear-rings bracelets have been found in male graves, both worn: Whitcombe, Dorset (grave 6: Whimster 1981: 271), Langton, N. Yorks. (Corder and Kirk 1932: 59, 66) and Cirencester (grave 179: McWhirr et al. 1982: 129); and unworn: Oakley Cottage, Cirencester (Reece 1962: 51).

Apart from being purely decorative, bracelets could secure amulets around the wrist, as at Cirencester (Crummy 1983: no. 1610) – where should the line be drawn between a bracelet worn for aesthetic reasons and something worn in order to fasten an amulet into position?

Finger rings are very difficult to attribute to a male or female wearer unless they are found *in situ* on a finger. Size alone is not an adequate criterion: some women have large hands, some men very small hands, and the wearing of rings on the second joint of the finger confuses the issue. It has often been supposed that only men wore intaglio rings but this is not so. Intaglios could be worn for decoration alone and women would also have required them for business purposes such as sealing letters and documents.

Jewellery, therefore, is not as clear an indicator of gender as might be thought.

A survey of the small finds from the turrets on Hadrian's Wall revealed other artefacts, which had traditionally been taken to be female, in male contexts (Allason-Jones 1988). The turrets were only occupied for a total of forty years in two separate stages and only by the military. None so far excavated show any sign of squatter occupation and several were either demolished or had their doorways blocked up when the army withdrew. It might, therefore, be presumed with some safety that only men attached to the army were present on these sites. The presence of needles, nail cleaners and tweezers – all traditionally used as indicators of a female presence – may come as a surprise. Soldiers in the 2nd century, no doubt, had to mend their clothes, clean their nails, and remove splinters. Recent excavations at Vindolanda and Carlisle show that Roman soldiers, like British soldiers in the Second World War and in the modern army, were issued with sewing kits – known nowadays as 'housewives'.

Among the commonest finds on Roman sites, whether civilian or military, are pins, made from a variety of materials. These artefacts have been the subject of a number of articles, both classifying the types and debating their use. MacGregor (1976: 13) expressed doubts as to whether they could all be identified as hairpins, offering an alternative suggestion that they were used to fasten garments. Cool, in 1991, presented the evidence for decorated pins having been solely for hairdressing, but the large number of roughly fashioned, undecorated, bone pins found on sites remain ambiguous. Philpott (1991) in discussing the possibility of attributing function to pins by their position in graves, emphasised the difficulties that ensue when the exact position is not recorded but drew attention to groups of pins found at the feet of inhumations. He pointed out that metal pins 'are rarely found close to the skull but are usually found lower down the body'. He continued, 'it may be significant that the deposition of metal pins which were apparently functional in the grave occurs at a time when there is a decline in the use of brooches in graves for fastening garments. Metal pins may have partially replaced brooches as shroud pins in the 3rd and perhaps 4th century' (1991: 151).

Much is known of hair fashions during the Roman period and while it is clear that both long and short hairpins were used, indeed required, in female hairstyles, there is no evidence that male hairstyles needed pinning. The Italian fashion was for men to wear their hair short and while male skeletons have been found with long hair in the Celtic provinces, for example at Poundbury (Green, Paterson and Biek 1981), none appear to have affected pins. We must, therefore, remain open minded as to whether the discovery of pins indicates a female presence.

So are there any groups of artefacts which clearly indicate the presence of women? Few seem to be good indicators – medical instruments with a purely gynaecological purpose form a rare group. There is also the possibility that items made of jet had special significance for women.

Jet was first worked in Britain in the Bronze Age but, although the Romans were aware of the properties of jet when they invaded Britain, the manufacture of jet objects at such places as York does not appear to have gathered momentum until the late 3rd or early 4th century. It was then used to make jewellery – beads, betrothal pendants, bracelets and fine finger rings, as well as hairpins, spindles, and spindlewhorls.

Jet is rarely found in a male grave in Britain and when it is, as at Oakley Cottage, Cirencester (Reece 1962: 51), it is unworn. Jet artefacts regularly appear in female graves at York and elsewhere in the country – mostly in the eastern counties. Knife handles and a few fragments of furniture inlay have also been found but these may have belonged to women. One clearly male item is the scabbard chape from Bonn in Germany (Hagen 1937) but this stands out as an exception, the rest all appearing to be biased towards the female.

The reasons for this bias may be religious as most of the British finds have been from graves or other religious contexts, or because jet, like amber, had a particular significance for women. Pliny related that 'the kindling of jet drives off snakes and relieves suffocation of the uterus. Its fumes detect attempts to simulate a disabling illness or a state of virginity' (*Nat. Hist.* XXXVI: 141–42). There is, however, a noticeable lack of fertility amulets made from jet.

So where does this leave Coventina's Well and Housesteads? The 'trinkets' from the Well include ten brooches, fourteen finger rings, two hairpins and five bracelets. These are the only objects which might be regarded as female on traditional criteria other than a large number of glass beads, all of which may be from the same necklace as they include twenty-four gold-in-glass beads. Coventina herself is unambiguously female (Allason-Jones and McKay 1985: pl. VI) although we have no clear evidence as to her responsibilities and one must conclude that she was an 'all-rounder', dealing with matters of healing among other human concerns. All the inscriptions refer to male worshippers, but this may not be significant in itself as women very rarely dedicated stonework to a deity on their own behalf – the ratio of female dedicators to male in Roman Britain being about 1 in 10. Are the pieces of jewellery the female equivalent of an altar dedicated by a man or would it be considered logical to present a female deity with a feminine artefact – an item of jewellery might be seen to be an appropriate offering with which to placate a female deity. There are no *ex votos* which might indicate a female congregation, unlike the spring of Sulis Minerva at Bath where breasts of ivory and bronze have been found (Cunliffe 1988: pl. 3). The Wheelers suggested that the discovery of hairpins and bracelets at a temple indicated a shrine of healing which catered for women with gynaecological complaints (Wheeler and Wheeler 1932: 42), but Coventina's Well with only five bracelets and two hairpins compares badly with the suggested temple of healing at Piercebridge, Co. Durham, where over one hundred of each have been found (Scott forthcoming).

The artefacts which might be regarded as male are also unimpressive: a strap-end, three studs, a seal-box, three belt buckles and seven bell-shaped studs. Of these, only the buckles can be regarded as being exclusively male with any confidence on the grounds that articles of female clothing of Roman date involving buckles have not been discovered so far. Having said that, women may have had buckled satchels, boxes or horse harness. The finds from Coventina's Well do not conclusively prove female devotees for the cult, whether love-lorn or not.

As was mentioned earlier, the jewellery from Housesteads found in barrack block XIII was considered proof of married quarters in the late 3rd century to the early 4th century. It was said that there was 'a preponderance of brooches and other trinkets'. The actual numbers of artefacts are twelve brooches, only two of which are of late 3rd to 4th century date, four finger rings, three bracelets, two ear-rings, and nine hairpins. This does not seem excessive when compared to other sites, particularly as the area of XIII covers the road outside as well as the interior of the building. The same picture emerges at Wallsend, where chalets have also been found (Daniels forthcoming). Wallsend has been almost fully uncovered and for the whole site there are forty-two brooches of which four are late; there are also ten bracelets, two ear-rings, six finger rings and thirty-six bone hairpins. Again, this does not imply a preponderance. Neither Housesteads nor Wallsend has produced much jet. If these two factors are added to the difficulty of ascribing artefacts to gender, the argument of the chalets being married quarters on finds evidence alone is considerably weakened.

This has been a brisk survey of only a small group of artefacts but it should serve as a warning about the dangers of identifying objects and their purpose from the limited viewpoint of modern values. The blinkered view of the predominantly male, middle class, 19th century archaeologist is still alive and well and even the most radical theorists can fall into the trap of building their theory on the shifting sands of small find identification.

Bibliography

Allason-Jones, Lindsay 1988. Small Finds from the Turrets on Hadrian's Wall. In J. C. Coulston (ed.), *Military Equipment and the Identity of Roman Soldiers,* 197–233. Oxford: British Archaeological Reports (IS 394).

Allason-Jones, Lindsay 1989a. *Ear-rings in Roman Britain.* Oxford: British Archaeological Reports (201).

Allason-Jones, Lindsay 1989b. *Women in Roman Britain.* London: British Museum Publications.

Allason-Jones, Lindsay and Bruce McKay, 1985. *Coventina's Well: A Shrine on Hadrian's Wall.* Chesters: Trustees of the Clayton Collection.

Anderson, J. 1904. A Note on a Late Keltic Armlet of Bronze, now Presented to the National Museum. *Proceedings of the Society of Antiquaries of Scotland* 38:460–466.

Bowman, Alan 1990. *Egypt after the Pharaohs.* London: Oxford University Press.

Bowman, Alan and J. David Thomas, 1986. Vindolanda 1985: the New Writing Tablets. *Journal of Roman Studies* 76:120–123.

Breeze, David and Brian Dobson, 1978. *Hadrian's Wall.* London: Penguin.

Charlton, D. Beryl and John Day, 1984. The Roman Cemetery at Petty Knowes, Rochester, Northumberland. *Archaeologia Aeliana* (5th series) 12:1–31.

Clarke, Giles 1979. *Pre-Roman and Roman Winchester.* Oxford: Oxford University Press.

Clayton, John 1880. Description of Roman Remains Discovered near to Procolitia, a Station on the Wall of Hadrian. *Archaeologia Aeliana* (2nd series) 8:1–39.

Cool, Hilary E. M. 1991. Roman Metal Hairpins from Southern Britain. *Archaeological Journal* 147 (1990):148–182.

Corder, Philip and J. L. Kirk, 1932. *A Roman Villa at Langton, near Malton, E. Yorkshire.* Leeds.

Coulston, Jon. C. and E. J. Phillips, 1988. *Corpus Signorum Imperii Romani: Great Britain, I.6, Hadrian's Wall West of the North Tyne and Carlisle.* Oxford: British Academy.

Crummy, Nina 1983. *Colchester Archaeological Report, 2, The Roman Small Finds from Excavations in Colchester 1971–9.* Colchester: Colchester Archaeological Trust.

Cunliffe, Barry 1988. *The Temple of Sulis Minerva at Bath, 2, The Finds from the Sacred Spring.* Oxford: Oxford Committee for Archaeology.

Daniels, Charles M. 1980. Excavation at Wallsend and the Fourth Century Barracks on Hadrian's Wall. In William S. Hanson and Lawrence J. F. Keppie (eds), *Roman Frontier Studies 1979,* 173–194.

Daniels, Charles M. forthcoming. Excavation Report on the Roman Fort at Wallsend.

Espérandieu, E. 1922. *Receuil général des bas-reliefs, statues et bustes de la Gaul Romaine.* Paris.

Frere, Sheppard S. and J. K. St. Joseph, 1974. The Roman Fortress at Long-thorpe. *Britannia* 5:1–129.

Green, C. S., M. Paterson and Leo Biek, 1981. A Roman Coffin-Burial from the Crown Buildings, Dorchester, with Particular Reference to the Head of Well Preserved Hair. *Proceedings of the Dorset Natural History and Archaeology Society* 103:67–100.

Hagen, Wilhelmine 1937. Kaiserzeitliche Gagatarbeiten aus den Rheinisches Germania. *Bonner Jahrbücher* 142:77–144.

Johns, Catherine, F. Hugh Thompson and P. Wagstaffe, 1981. The Wincle, Cheshire, Hoard of Roman Gold Jewellery. *Antiquaries Journal* 60:48–58.

Maxfield, Valerie A. 1974. The Benwell Torc – Roman or Native? *Archaeologia Aeliana* (5th series) 2:41–48.

McGregor, A. 1976. *Finds from a Roman Sewer System and an Adjacent Building in Church Street, York.* York: York Archaeological Trust.

McWhirr, Alan, Linda Viner and Calvin Wells, 1982. *Romano-British Cemeteries at Cirencester: Cirencester Excavations II.* Cirencester: Cirencester Excavation Committee.

Philpott, Robert 1991. *Burial Practices in Roman Britain.* Oxford: British Archaeological Reports (219).

Reece, Richard 1962. The Oakley Cottage Romano-British Cemetery, Cirencester. *Transactions of the Bristol and Gloucester Archaeol. Society* 81:51–72.

Scott, Peter R. forthcoming. Excavation Report on the Roman Fort at Piercebridge.

Shotter, David C. A. 1973a. *Romans in Lancashire.* Clapham: Dalesman Books.

Shotter, David C. A. 1973b. *Numeri Barcariorum*: a Note on RIB 601. *Britannia* 4:206–209.

Toynbee, Jocelyn M. C. 1978. *Roman Historical Portraits.* London: Thames and Hudson.

Wheeler, R. E. Mortimer and Tessa V. Wheeler, 1932. *Report on the Excavations of the Prehistoric Roman and Post Roman Site in Lydney Park, Gloucestershire.* Oxford: Society of Antiquaries of London.

Whimster, Rowan 1981. *Burial Practices in Iron Age Britain: a Discussion and Gazetteer of the Evidence, c. 700 BC – AD 43.* Oxford: British Archaeological Reports (90).

Wild, John Peter 1968. Clothing in the North-West Provinces of the Roman Empire. *Bonner Jahrbücher* 168:166–240.

3

ROMAN FINDS ASSEMBLAGES, TOWARDS AN INTEGRATED APPROACH?

Jeremy Evans

Since this paper was to be given to a Theoretical Roman Archaeology conference an attempt has been made here to examine a little the relationship between theoretical approaches and the generally pragmatic work of field archaeology in the context of Roman finds assemblages. It is assumed for the purposes of this paper that our basic task as archaeologists is to examine and analyse Romano-British society by means of reasoning about its material remains.

It does seem to this author, from his own basically pragmatic viewpoint, that there is a rather over-wide gulf between the development and propounding of theories on Romano-British archaeology and the day to day business of its recording and reporting, which in part reflects a division between those employed in Universities and those working in field archaeology. These might perhaps be crassly described as the 'two cultures' of Romano-British archaeology. This is not to denigrate theoretical approaches to Romano-British archaeology, they seem desperately needed as we acquire more and more data, but seem to get bogged-down in recording it, without the commensurate expansion of our understanding of the general processes taking place in Roman Britain.

Rather it seems to this author that theoretical approaches are generally too divorced from the material evidence and that, in turn, is often presented in manners which do not aid its synthetic analysis. It seems far too rarely that theories are tested against the evidence, which they usually can be either directly, or by deduction of their material consequences were they to be true and then seeking these. It is recognised that the testing of theories will be a Bayesian process, where they may not be completely refuted, but they can at least be considerably weakened by failing to be consistent with the evidence.

This author's concern here is not to set about doing this, but to look at the other side of the equation, that mass of data that we spend much of our professional lives accumulating, and to suggest some lines of enquiry we might consider developing and a general approach which might facilitate the examination of theoretical approaches.

THE SAMPLE ————

Turning to our data, the first point to be made is that we select a very odd collection of sites from which to study the diocese. Most authorities estimate that around 90% of the population lived on rural sites, in villages or isolated settlements, but these seem to have evoked little interest and stimulated disproportionately few excavations and fieldwork projects compared with forts, towns and villas. Table 3.1 shows the numbers of rural sites excavated as a proportion of all excavations recorded in Britannia since 1970. Only excavations have been counted and those have been counted by the year, so that sites with several seasons of excavation will have multiple records. Most of the site classes are self-explanatory; 'other' principally comprises pottery kilns and temples. Excavations of field systems have not been counted, nor have the too frequent trenches across Roman roads.

Table 3.1. The incidence of excavations on Roman sites by site type and Britannia region (see Fig. 3.1).

	1969–1973								
Region	I	II	III	IV	V	VI	VII	VIII	IX
Site type									
Fort	60%	81%	62%	30%	12%	6%	0	6%	10%
Vicus	0	9%	15%	10%	0	0	0	0	0
Hillfort	7%	6%	0	0	0	0	0	0	1%
Town	5%	0	0	23%	27%	41%	60%	29%	30%
Villa	5%	0	0	15%	22%	10%	4%	23%	28%
Rural	14%	3%	21%	11%	21%	19%	8%	34%	17%
Other	10%	0	3%	11%	17%	25%	28%	9%	15%
n	42	32	39	133	180	69	25	101	178

1974–78

Region	I	II	III	IV	V	VI	VII	VIII	IX
Site type									
Fort	49%	70%	55%	36%	8%	0	2%	14%	8%
Vicus	12%	15%	0	7%	1%	2%	0	1%	2%
Hillfort	2%	0	0	0	0	0	0	1%	0
Town	14%	0	21%	25%	41%	45%	76%	33%	30%
Villa	2%	0	0	9%	15%	5%	7%	22%	21%
Rural	14%	15%	18%	15%	25%	28%	2%	10%	18%
Other	7%	0	5%	7%	11%	22%	13%	15%	20%
n	43	47	38	151	165	65	46	72	142

1979–1983

Region	I	II	III	IV	V	VI	VII	VIII	IX
Site type									
Fort	37%	85%	76%	32%	12%	3%	0	15%	4%
Vicus	2%	3%	0	15%	1%	0	0	3%	2%
Hillfort	7%	9%	0	1%	1%	0	0	3%	2%
Town	29%	0	21%	21%	30%	46%	84%	20%	22%
Villa	7%	0	0	12%	15%	5%	4%	18%	26%
Rural	19%	3%	0	14%	27%	26%	2%	21%	21%
Other	0	0	3%	5%	15%	21%	10%	20%	22%
n	59	33	33	108	122	39	49	80	134

1984–1988

Region	I	II	III	IV	V	VI	VII	VIII	IX
Site type									
Fort	45%	93%	89%	37%	12%	9%	1%	8%	3%
Vicus	21%	3%	7%	11%	1%	2%	0	1%	1%
Hillfort	3%	0	0	4%	1%	2%	0	0	0
Town	18%	0	0	23%	30%	42%	73%	41%	42%
Villa	3%	0	0	2%	19%	5%	5%	25%	26%
Rural	7%	3%	4%	19%	19%	22%	0	14%	15%
Other	3%	0	0	12%	19%	20%	20%	11%	14%
n	62	29	28	91	108	65	79	92	122

1969–89

Region	I	II	III	IV	V	VI	VII	VIII	IX	All
Site type										
Fort	47%	82%	71%	33%	11%	4%	1%	10%	6%	21%
Vicus	9%	8%	4%	11%	1%	1%	0	1%	1%	4%
Hillfort	5%	3%	0	1%	0%	0%	0	1%	1%	1%
Town	18%	0	11%	23%	32%	42%	75%	53%	31%	31%
Villa	4%	0	0	10%	18%	7%	5%	22%	25%	14%
Rural	13%	7%	11%	13%	24%	24%	3%	20%	18%	17%
Other	4%	0	3%	8%	15%	22%	16%	13%	18%	13%
n	210	146	140	511	589	247	210	356	607	3016

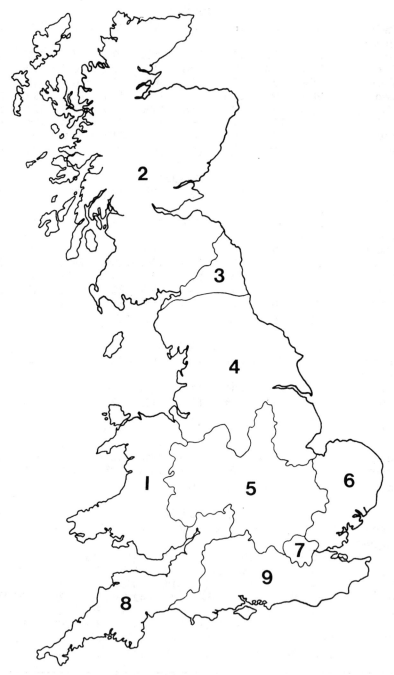

Figure 3.1. Map of the regions by which Britannia *reports excavations.*

Table 3.1 shows the data split into four blocks of five years and together as a twenty one year block. There are marked regional variations, and some shifts of emphasis with time, but the first point to emerge is that rural sites are grossly under-represented, overall comprising only 16.7% of the sites listed. This global figure hides some fairly consistent regional variations. Regions I-IV, ie Wales, Scotland, Hadrian's Wall and northern England are the regions in which rural sites are the most poorly represented, apart from London (for which the reasons are fairly obvious). The home counties, region IX, also has a fairly poor representation of rural sites, whilst the best regions are V, VI, and VII, the Midlands, East Anglia and the south-west. Worryingly the chronological trend seems to be against the excavation of rural sites; in 1969–73, 1974–78 and 1979–83 they formed 18% of all excavations reported, but in the following quinquennium, 1984–88, they fall to a mere 13% of excavations.

The totals of excavated sites shown in Table 3.1 reflect subjective perceptions of the impact of public expenditure policies since the later 1970s, falling from 799 in 1969–73 to 769 in 1974–78 and to 657 in 1979–83 with a slight rise to 676 in 1984–88 reflecting the rise of developer funding. It is clear from the figures, too, that the benefits of developer funding have been confined almost entirely to the Midlands and the south, adding further regional bias to our national sample. The Welsh Office (region I) seems to manage things better with a rise in the number of excavations from 1969–1988, whilst the number of Scots sites excavated in 1984–88 was only slightly fewer than in 1969–73.

Fulford (pers. comm.) rightly points out that these data on excavation numbers do not necessarily reflect the expenditure on excavations on different site types and evidence of this would be interesting (although difficult to obtain including developer funded excavations).

The reluctance to excavate rural sites must reflect the attitudes of funding bodies and the planning processes which tend to assess the importance of sites as individual units, without full regard to the development of research strategies which might elucidate more of the economy, social relations and identity of the rural population, and of its relationships to 'urban' and 'villa' centres. As an example of this tendency the number of fort excavations, 21% of all sites, compared with excavations of *vici*, 4% of all sites, suggests that Roman military archaeology still lacks interest in the civilian communities associated with forts.

QUESTIONS AND APPROACHES ————

Despite the devotion of a series of volumes to the *civitates* of Roman Britain we still know little of what are the material cultures of the diocese. The *civitas* volumes seem to have paid more attention to piecemeal chunks of the history and pseudo-history of the diocese than to examining material (culture) patterning within and across cantonal and regional boundaries. Interesting patterns would seem to exist in the evidence, take, for example, the division of the Dobunni into three groups on the basis of their coinage (Selwood 1989: fig 13.11), and the inclusion of the southern of these in the core distribution of BB1 types (which rarely, if ever, travel to the Midlands, Wales or the north), and the concentration of most hall villas within the Dobunnic territory as defined by Selwood (Millett 1990: fig. 87; note the *civitas* boundaries on this do not correspond with Selwood's). There are also enormous differences in the finds assemblages between highland and lowland zone sites (see below).

THE RECORD ————

Turning to the published archaeological record, much is said of archaeological reporting as preservation by record, but the record, as compared with the material and stratigraphic archive, is frequently incomplete and often delphic. As with pottery reports 25 years ago, many finds reports consist of detailed descriptions and parallels of individual objects of 'intrinsic interest', but with no indication of whether some, all, or a 'representative selection' of the particular type has been made (or of how much the editor has removed).

Pottery reports have slowly become quantified, or rather pottery fabrics are fairly often quantified relative to each other in publications, following Young's (1980) guidelines. This has been a fairly slow process, however, Griffiths (1989: 67) commented 'Exhaustive enquiries revealed that nowhere on the continent or in Britain could all these criteria be satisfied [of holding the data in consistent format required for her study]. Of the five most likely areas in Britain, only two local units could supply a consolidated form/fabric series for their local coarsewares, only one of which was available for immediate use in 1982 when these enquiries were made. The publication record for recent excavations was overall fairly good, but the almost total lack of quantification, even on sites published since 1980, was surprising.' Even when quantification has been done, and has included the samian ware and mortaria, it is frequently impossible to discover how many vessels of which form occur in which phase. Sometimes pottery reports may be fully quantified, but very rarely is it then possible to establish how many, of which finds types, occur with the pottery. An excellent example of this is the good series of published pottery groups from a number of different rural and villa sites in the environs of Milton Keynes (Marney 1989). It would be of interest in the light of these and their use by Griffiths (1989) to quantify the glassware assemblages from the same groups against the proportion of fineware and to examine other aspects of the finds assemblages. However, the full glass report by Price (1987) has been edited: 'owing to limitations of space only the more interesting pieces have been described below' (Mynard 1987). Further analysis from the published record is therefore impossible, despite the use of microfiche in the volume, which one might expect to obviate such limitations. It is unclear which other finds categories have been dealt a similar fate.

Fulford (1975: 134) has suggested that the absolute quantity of pottery on Roman sites, especially in the south-east, may have been declining in the later fourth century. This is, in principle, a testable hypothesis, with interesting implications for assertions made about the later Roman economy. Unfortunately the test would require a record, or reasonably accurate estimate, of the volume of earth relative to the quantity of excavated pottery from an acceptable sample of sites, but to this author's knowledge, this information has been recorded on only two Romano-British excavations, Lynch Farm (Jones 1977) and Shipton Thorpe, even though this was done on the former in 1977! No doubt, inter alia, excavators are deterred from doing this by the knowledge that it is a tool of comparative method, and that without any other sites with which to compare their data they can do little with it apart from publishing and hoping that someone else will benefit. An analogous situation seems to have existed with pottery assemblages, where, following Hull's (1932) quantified report on the Yorkshire signal stations further quantified reports followed on late Roman assemblages (Gillam 1957; Corder 1961) but not on any earlier material.

What seems to be lacking in many published reports is any coherent philosophy of preservation by record. Instead the finds assemblage is fragmented into large numbers of individual specialist reports, but the finds officer/excavator responsible for collecting these makes little attempt to put them together again and examine trends in the assemblage as a whole. Thus the basic aim of the reconstructability of the assemblage from the record is often lost, despite the advent of microfiche which should

allow reconstructability at reasonable cost. (Even if microfiche is an outdated technology that would be better replaced by read-only ASCII com-
puter discs and printed drawings (cf. Hen Domen: Barker and Higham
1982).

It now seems that it is not only reports published some time ago to which
Pitt-Rivers (1887: xvii) comments are applicable:

> Excavators, as a rule, record only those things which appear to
> them important at the time, but fresh problems in Archaeology and
> Anthropology are constantly arising, and it can hardly fail to escape
> the notice of anthropologists . . . that on turning back to old
> accounts in search of evidence, the points which would have been
> most valuable have been passed over from being thought un-
> interesting at the time. Every detail should, therefore be recorded
> in the manner most conducive to facility of reference.

The omens are still not too good as it appears that the basic ceramic evidence from urban sequences is supposed to be replaced by ceramic (only)
syntheses (Fulford and Huddlestone 1991). It also appeared that assessments of the post-excavation treatment of finds groups were likely to be
made on a material by material basis (Wainwright 1990), or, if not, then
only the more exceptional (and therefore atypical) groups were liable to be
funded, although this emphasis seems now to have been modified (Wainwright 1991a: appendix 4, section 4.2.1.ii). However, nowhere in *The
Management of Archaeological Projects* 2 (Wainwright 1991a) is any commitment made to the reconstructability of the assemblage and the general
system still appears to be designed to avoid publishing 'uninteresting' finds
and the danger of this has been emphasised by the recent Society of Antiquaries discussion paper on archives and publication.

One of the reasons that the data are treated as they are may be that there
is still little of an archaeology of Roman Britain in the sense of an interpretation of it based primarily on the material record rather than inspired by
history or 'pseudo-history'. Millett (1990) noted that 'during the work on
this book I have become intensely aware that some established opinions
about the subject are based not on evidence, but on what have been called
'factoids'. These are pieces of information which have been so commonly
repeated that they are almost indistinguishable from facts.' Interpretation
in Romano-British archaeology is rarely 'firmly based in material and in the
demonstrated relationships between different parts of that material' (Reece
1988). Lacking the basic data we tend to assert its nature on the basis of im-

pressions and then go on to interpret these.

Collingwood (1946: 149) commented:

> 'History' said Bury 'is a science, no less and no more.' There is a slang usage . . . according to which 'science' means natural science. Whether history is a science in that sense of the word, however, need not be asked; for in the tradition of European speech going back to the time when Latin speakers translated the Greek *episteme* by their own word *scientia*, and continuing unbroken down to the present day, the word 'science' means any organized body of knowledge. If that is what the word means Bury is so far incontestably right, that history is a science, nothing less.

He went on to say (1946: 251):

> History then, is a science, but a science of a special kind. It is a science whose business is to study events not accessible to our observation, and to study these events inferentially, arguing to them from something else which is accessible to our observation, and which the historian calls 'evidence' for the events in which he is interested.

In both of these quotations archaeology could, with little modification, be substituted for history, but in large part a 'scientific archaeology' of Roman Britain has yet to develop and the phrase is generally employed for the piecemeal use of techniques borrowed from the natural sciences. The study of data to observe trends for which interpretations might be advanced and tested against further data is hampered enormously by the lack of fully and consistently published data.

INTEGRATED APPROACHES ———

This section is drawn principally from data easily at hand and does not purport to be a review. Its aim is to illustrate some types of approach and to sketch one or two possible trends in data which might repay further study.

Volume of excavated earth figures do exist for a Norman to post-medieval sequence from the Orange Grove excavations in Bath (O'Leary 1981; Evans and Millett 1992). Figure 3.2 shows the number of roughly contemporary and Roman residual sherds per cubic metre in the medieval sequence from these excavations and the numbers of roughly contempor-

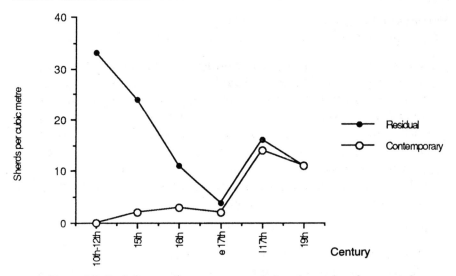

Figure 3.2. Bath Orange Grove pottery supply by volume of earth excavated (after Evans and Millett 1992).

ary and Roman and medieval residual sherds in the post-medieval part of the sequence. The sequence does offer some interesting possibilities with the absolute quantity of Roman material being much greater than medieval. Even in the late seventeenth century in this sequence Roman residual material is commoner than medieval residual sherds. This could merely be a product of the nature of this specific sequence where the Roman occupation was probably an intensively used area as it is less than 150m from the spring, whilst the medieval site consisted of the Abbey foundations and a cemetery and the post-medieval one was a public park.

One reason why the Bath sequence might reflect a more general trend comes from a functional analysis of the material from all periods (Evans 1985: tables 5.14 and 5.15) following the definitions used on Roman material by Millett (1979) and Evans (1985). There is clearly much less functional diversity in the medieval assemblage than amongst the Roman one and this diversity is only restored in the post-medieval period. A similar pattern can be seen in the similar analyses of a sequence from Chester-le-Street, Co. Durham (Evans 1991) and the medieval to post-medieval sequence from the Newcastle Castle ditch (Ellison 1981). The lack of functional diversity in medieval assemblages emphasises the point, more easily accepted for aceramic periods, that pottery is employed for a different range of activities in different periods, and if the range is comparatively restricted the absolute quantity in use may well be less.

A further point emerges from these three medieval to post-medieval sequences from the function figures (and from the sequences of basic technology (handmade/wheelmade/moulded) and surface treatment (glaze type)). Developments seem to take place earliest in the Newcastle sequence, followed by the Bath one, with Chester-le-Street trailing behind, this would seem to reflect the social and economic status of the sites, a castle in a major 'port of trade', a prosperous southern town, and a back street site in a minor market town (cf. Weatherill 1988).

An interesting attempt to integrate interpretation of the finds assemblage from a site was made by Halstead, Hodder and Jones (1979), who utilised both variations in the levels of ceramic finewares and the classes of bone waste, examining these in relation to the types of features excavated and their spatial distribution. The authors concluded that 'though in the Iron Age there is little remaining evidence of spatial separation of activities on the site, past separation of activities in space and/or time resulted in segregation of different types of refuse. This is less the case in the larger more complex Roman site where there is more mixture of different types of rubbish' (Halstead et al. 1979: 130).

A similar study, regrettably unpublished, was made of the well and pit groups at Portchester utilising data on the principal pottery fabrics, fineware levels, functional groupings of the small finds and a rather more sophisticated division of the animal bone assemblage than that employed at Wendens Ambo (Creighton 1985). Consistent differences were demonstrated between the pit groups, characterised by a more industrial use, and the isolated pits and wells receiving domestic debris. This, together clearly defined discrete pit complexes, suggested a high degree of zoned activity on the site, consistent with a well-organised, presumably military, occupation (Creighton 1985: section 6). Interestingly, this is the second re-examination of these features, the first being by Millett (1979), which seems to reflect not weaknesses in the original report but rather its usefulness in providing the full data necessary for subsequent re-evaluation.

Figure 3.3 (Evans forthcoming b) shows the ratio of various common finds types relative to the quantity of pottery from the Roman fort at Segontium: the numbers of nails, tile fragments and bone fragments divided by the number of sherds of pottery. Figure 3.4 shows a similar diagram, calculated on the same basis, for three third century sequences from Gas House Lane, Alcester (Evans forthcoming c) and one of the later fourth century. Ideally the figures would be best standardised by the

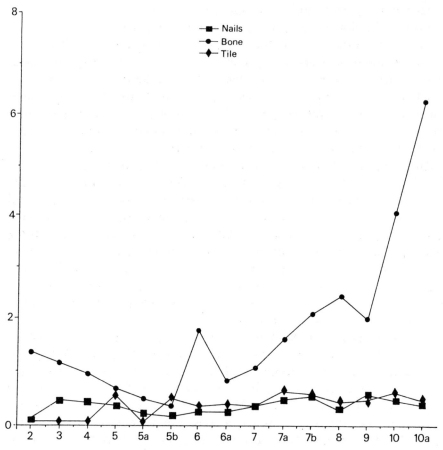

*Figure 3.3. Ratio of common finds types by period
at Segontium relative to the quantity of pottery.*

volume of deposits excavated, but, this information was not available. Standardisation by the quantity of pottery does assume that, overall, the amount of pottery and the way it was discarded was similar in all parts of the Roman period, not an entirely reliable assumption. However, if the quantity of pottery is the main factor changing between phases then all three of the ratios being examined should change together. In fact in the Segontium sequence the data all change together only in period 7A, for which a fall in the quantity of pottery could be suggested.

Various interesting details appear in the Segontium sequence (Evans forthcoming b) such as in the apparent demolition debris (period 5A) of

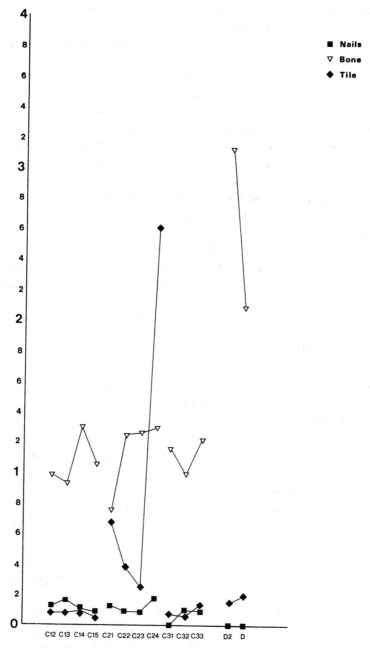

Figure 3.4. Ratio of common finds types by period at Alcester, Gas House Land, relative to the quantity of pottery.

the period 5 structures, which appears to represent a dump of outdated material, especially samian (King and Millett forthcoming) also contains fairly few nails, and very little tile. This seems to suggest that nails, and perhaps tile, were deliberately stripped from the building on demolition. But there is a fairly consistent change in the sequence from period 6, with the amount of animal bone rising sharply. The greater quantities of bone may reflect a change in waste disposal practices, which would not have needed to be as strict as previously since the population density of the area had fallen very considerably. Periods 6A and 7 are fairly similar to 6, but period 7A saw an increase in both bone, tile and nails. This could reflect a fall in the quantity of pottery in period 7A, but given structural evidence suggesting that the period 7 courtyard building was rather run down in this period a real increase in the quantity of refuse left around would seem likely.

The amount of bone further increases in period 7B, which is satisfactorily similar to period 8 with which it is at least partly contemporary. The quantity of bone continued to increase in period 10, no doubt from the back-filling of the pits with domestic waste, and there is a further rise in period 10A with domestic waste being dumped in the large disused drain across the site.

The Gas House Lane sequence (Fig. 3.4) shows similar basic trends to the Segontium one for the 3rd and 4th centuries. As in the former sequence all three third century sequences show a bone fragment to pottery ratio fluctuating around 1:1, this seems to be quite a general phenomenon (compare the 'Romanised' sites on Fig. 3.7). The quantity of tile in the sequences tends to suggest its use on the site from its inception and the proportion of nails seems to remain fairly constant. The only really notable deviations in the tile figures are in phases C21 and especially in phase C23. This latter was the only point in the third century sequences where *pilae* occur and it appears that a hypocaust has been demolished or refurbished somewhere in the vicinity of the site. The late fourth century groups from area A, phase D2, and phase D, dating to after c. AD 370 show an interesting change. The lack of nails no doubt reflects the lack of buildings in the areas with phase D deposits (whether in this phase or earlier) although there are quantities of tile, perhaps dumped along with quantities of domestic waste. The quantity of bone has risen markedly, as in the Segontium sequence, if not as greatly. In both these cases it is suggested that this phenomenon reflects a breakdown in previous waste disposal practices at this period. Similar changes can also be seen elsewhere: the tip of late Roman domestic waste on the berm outside the city wall in Lincoln (Darling 1977) or the large spread of late fourth century material around the buildings and yard of the villa at Beadlam, North Yorks. (Stead 1971); and the large deposit including several pole-axed cattle skulls from the partially demolished *prae-furnium* of the later fourth century hypocaust of the 'Commandant's House' of the fort at Binchester, Co. Durham.

It is possible to see these figures as reflecting Fulford's (1975) suggestion that the absolute quantities of Roman pottery was in decline in the late fourth century. However, given that the quantity of pottery from period 10A at Segontium was very large, as it was from the Lincoln and Binchester deposits cited above this seems unlikely, as such, although only volume figures will show this. It might be possible, however, that there is a dichotomy between deposits in northern and western England and those in the south-east, given other suggestions (see below) of there being two different ceramic cultures in these areas by the late fourth century.

Figures 3.5 and 3.6 show the proportions of finewares from assemblages from various sites of early-mid and late fourth century date from northern and southern England. The figures, in fact, are not quite comparable as the northern ones (Evans 1985) include painted parchment wares, one of the principal late fourth century finewares in the region, whilst the southern ones are restricted to colour-coated wares, thus the northern figures are slightly higher than they might be. It is, however, clear that whilst there is a slight rise in the proportion of finewares in the north in the later fourth century, this does not generally amount to a level greater than 15% and the maximum value is below 25%.

In the south in the early fourth century the fineware level seems to be on average more like 10–20% and on, many, but not all, sites the fineware level rises markedly in the late fourth century. The average level is probably in the order of 25%, but quite a number of sites produce levels over 40%. A similar effect may be observed by comparing Hodder's map of the proportions of samian ware (Millett 1990: fig. 54) from assemblages in the south-west with his maps of the proportions of 3rd and 4th century finewares from the same area (Hodder 1974: fig. 8). (As Fulford (pers. comm.) has rightly commented there are some sub-regional trends within the broad brush approach being taken here, and these may prove of interest when regional studies of finewares and site status are made.)

A similar dichotomy can be seen developing between north and south in the functional use of pottery. In the third century the level of jars on sites in the north (Evans 1985: table 5.2) seems to be similar to those in the

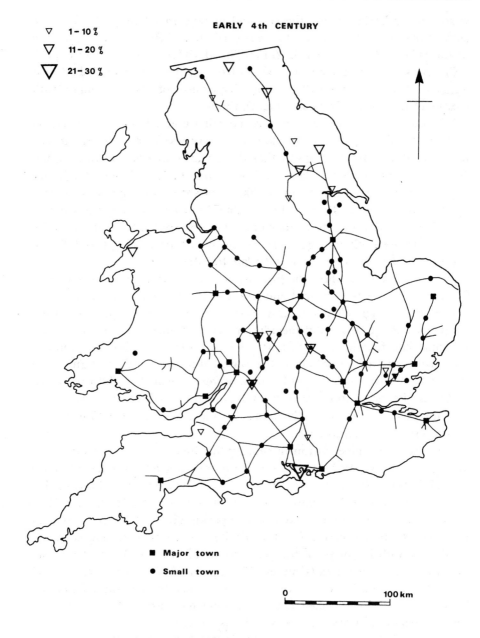

Figure 3.5. The proportions of finewares from various sites in the early fourth century.

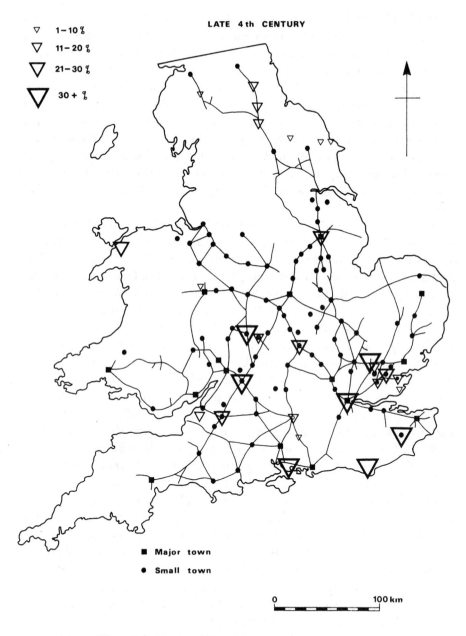

Figure 3.6. The proportions of finewares from various sites in the late fourth century.

south (Going 1987; Millett 1979; Millett 1983; Evans forthcoming c), but in
the early fourth century this rises slightly in the north to a general range of
40–50% and in the late fourth century there is a further rise to levels generally above 50% and often markedly so. Meanwhile in the south the proportion of jars often falls to its lowest level in the late fourth century as the proportion of tablewares increases with the proportion of finewares. (Again
some sub-regional trends may also be present such as the high levels of
drinking vessels on some Severn Valley region sites) (Evans forthcoming a).

Undoubtedly the two phenomena sketched out above (Evans in prep.)
deserve further study, but it seems that generally two different 'material
cultures' of ceramic use were developing in 'Roman' Britain in the late
fourth century.

Figures 3.7, 3.8 and 3.9 show the finds assemblages divided by basic
material types standardised to finds per square metre (in default of volume
figures this is believed to be a reasonable measure for sites without deep
stratigraphy) from Roman and early post-Roman sites. Figure 3.7 shows the
assemblages from six Roman rural sites, three, Elsted in West Sussex (Redknap and Millett 1980), Ower in Dorset (Sunter and Woodward 1987) and
Bradley Hill in Somerset (Leech 1982), from the lowland zone, Roman
Britain *proprii dictu*, and three, Milking Gap in Northumberland (Kilbride-
Jones 1938), Graeanog in Gwynedd (Kelly forthcoming) and Staden in
Derbyshire (Makepeace 1983) from the highland zone. Figure 3.8 in comparison shows the same data from three post-Roman sites, all with claims of
rather higher status than the above Roman sites: Cadbury-Congresbury,
Somerset, which has been suggested to be a monastic site (Fowler et al.
1970), Bantham, Devon, is interpreted as a port site (Silvester 1981) and
phase 3C at Cowdrey's Down, Hampshire (Millett 1983). (For the latter site
the area figures have been adjusted and only the roofed area of the settlement in this phase has been used.) Figure 3.9, for comparison, shows finds
from area 7 for four succeeding third century phases at the small town of
Alcester, Warwickshire. The deposits here are not deep, nor do they necessarily extend over the whole area of the trench in each phase and plotted
by phase they are felt to be reasonably comparable with the other data.

These figures, from which the rest of this paper arises, were constructed
to attempt to examine and illustrate differences in the finds assemblages
between Roman and post-Roman sites. The selection of the sites is reasonably random, the main constraints being the difficulty of finding out the
quantities of pottery and animal bone from sites and small finds reports
which appear to be complete, and sites which appear to have been reason-

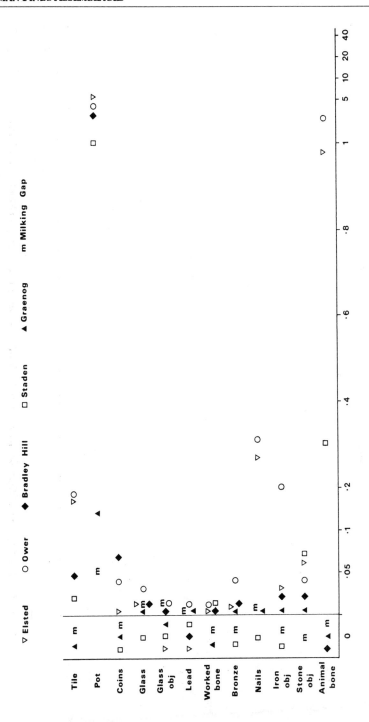

Figure 3.7. The frequency of finds occurrence standardised by site area from six Roman rural sites.

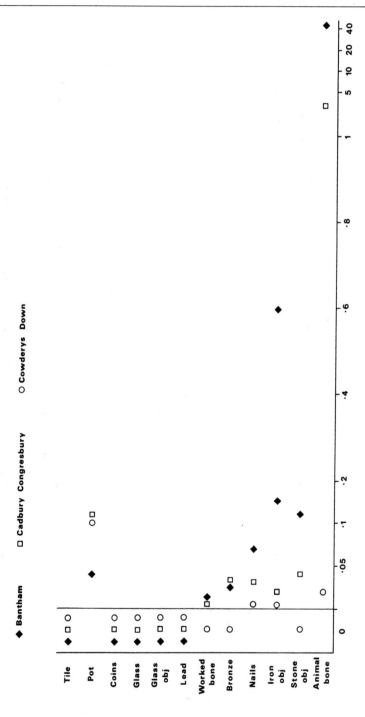

Figure 3.8. The frequency of finds occurrence standardised by site area from three post-Roman rural sites.

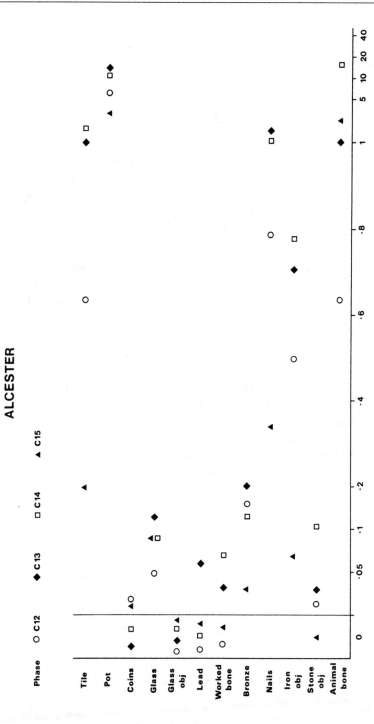

Figure 3.7. The frequency of finds occurrence standardised by site area from three phases at Gas House Lane, Alcester.

ably fully excavated within the limits of their trenches. Even so the number of nails from Bradley Hill is unreported as is the quantity of animal bone.

It is reasonably clear that the Roman lowland rural sites have much more pottery, as expected, but also more nails, sometimes more iron and definitely a wider range of material types than the post-Roman sites which were probably of a higher status. Figure 3.7 further emphasises the considerable material dichotomy between highland and lowland zone rural sites, the highland zone sites quite often having lower finds levels than on the post-Roman sites, although they do have a rather wider selection of finds classes and a little more pottery. Regional variations within highland zone sites in fact seem to be exhibited in the quantity of pottery, with Pennine and Cumbrian sites having very little, but those in North Wales, at least, having rather more (cf. Gidney 1986; Dore 1983; Going and Marsh forthcoming; Evans forthcoming d, e and f). Interestingly one of the four categories of finds types both highland and post-Roman sites tend to have more of than lowland Roman rural sites is stone artefacts, hones, whetstones, quernstones, etc., in part this is no doubt related to geological conditions, but also probably to the fact that this material type is available everywhere and does not necessarily rely on trade or exchange for its provision.

One interesting implication of this illustration of the highland/lowland division between 'Roman Britain' and the contemporary 'Celtic West', is in the role of the military *vici* in the 'Celtic West', especially in north-western England. These were clearly not centres providing goods and services for the surrounding countryside in the same way as such settlements, in Yorkshire for example. Leaving aside possible reasons for this, the simple lack of reasonable quantities of 'Romanised' goods on the rural sites demonstrates it. It is much more probable that the *vicani* formed an alien blot on the landscape, along with the forts (quite probably even speaking a different language from the surrounding rural population). The disappearance of these sites in the 4th century, compared with the continued occupation of such sites in Yorkshire until the end of the century is eloquent testimony to the differences of function between these sites in the two regions (Evans 1984).

The Alcester urban sequences, in contrast to those discussed above, might suggest that in the third century this small town may still have functioned as a central node for the distribution of goods, with much higher densities of finds and a wider range of finds types than on the rural sites examined. (This is not a consequence of residual material, the particular site being occupied de novo at this time).

It would seem from this sketchy and very preliminary survey that many data remain to be studied in comparative examination of the finds assemblages from Roman sites, however, Honorius's letter of AD 410, to Bruttium or Britain (Rivet and Smith 1979), is only the end of the world for Romanists and such comparisons with both early and high medieval sites (and even post-medieval sites) might prove revealing in a *longue durée* approach. Indeed it would seem to be in the early post-medieval period that many Roman type features of assemblages reappear, perhaps one of the benefits of the unseen hand of money taxation and government expenditure, rather than providence? (cf. Evans 1990; Pearce 1942; Hill 1980).

CONCLUSIONS ————

This paper has attempted to show that there is considerable scope for the development of the study of Roman finds assemblages and a Romano-British archaeology, but that one of the prerequisites for this is the capacity to express sites as a matrix of associated finds and that some method of absolute quantification such as the volume of earth excavated is needed. Volume figures are not a panacea, and will not necessarily provide the grounds for simple comparisons between groups: factors such as context type will also need to be taken into account. However, in the absence of data, the difficulties which may be encountered when they exist remain speculative. The ability to examine sites as a matrix of associated finds will not in itself solve any problems, but will provide a basis for the realistic comparison of, and the systematic examination of trends in, the archaeology. Hypotheses to explain patterning in the data might then be proposed and their material corollaries tested: a sine qua non for the development of a rigourous and mature archaeology, as opposed to a history or culture-history, of Roman Britain.

ACKNOWLEDGEMENTS ————

The author wishes to thank Chris Scull, Martin Millett and Mike Fulford for comments on drafts of this paper which have improved it considerably (particularly the former for his sterling work on the English). The author, however, remains solely responsible for the opinions expressed and all remaining errors. The illustrations are the work of Nigel Dodds and Steve Rigby.

Bibliography

Barker, Philip and R. Higham 1982. *Hen Domen, Montgomery*, v. 1. London: R.A.I.

Collingwood, Robin G. 1946. *The Idea of Nature*. Oxford: Oxford University Press.

Corder, Philip C. 1961. *The Roman Town and Villa at Great Casterton, Rutland*, Third Report.

Creighton, John 1985. Portchester Castle; an Investigation into the Analysis of Site Finds. Unpublished undergraduate dissertation, University of Durham.

Cunliffe, Barry and David Miles (eds), 1984. *Aspects of the Iron Age in Central Southern Britain*, 191–204. Oxford.

Darling, Maggi 1977. *A Group of Late Roman Pottery from Lincoln*. London: Council for British Archaeology (for Lincoln Archaeological Trust, 16.1).

Dore, John 1983. The Pottery. In Nicholas Higham and G. Barri D. Jones (eds), The Excavations of Two Romano-British Farm Sites in North Cumbria. *Britannia* 14:67–70.

Ellison, Anne 1981. The pottery. In Barbara Harbottle and Anne Ellison (eds), An Excavation in the Castle Ditch, Newcastle-upon-Tyne 1974–6. *Archaeologia Aeliana* (ser. 5) 9:95–164.

Evans, Jeremy 1984. Settlement and Society in North-Eastern England in the Fourth Century. In Peter Wilson, Richard F. J. Jones and David M. Evans (eds), *Settlement and Society in the Roman North*, 43–48. Bradford.

Evans, Jeremy 1990. From the End of Roman Britain to the 'Celtic West'. *Oxford Journal of Archaeology* 9.1:91–103.

Evans, Jeremy 1991. The Chester-le-Street Pottery. In Jeremy Evans, Richard F. J. Jones and Percival T. Turnbull (eds), Excavations at Chester-le-Street 1978–9. *Durham Arch. Journal* 6: fiche 83–130.

Evans, Jeremy forthcoming a. The Bidford Grange (BG91) Pottery. In Nicholas Palmer (ed.), Report on excavations at Bidford Grange, Warks. *Transactions of the Birmingham and Warwickshire Archaeological Society*.

Evans, Jeremy forthcoming b. The finds synthesis. In John Casey, John L. Davies and Jeremy Evans (eds), *Excavations at Segontium 1975–79*. London: Council for British Archaeology.

Evans, Jeremy forthcoming c. The Gas House Lane Pottery. In Stephen Cracknell (ed.), Excavations at Gas House Lane, Alcester. In Stephen Cracknell *Roman Alcester, 3, the Defended Area*. London: Council for British Archaeology.

Evans, Jeremy forthcoming d. The Graeanog Pottery. In Richard Kelly (ed.), Report on Excavations at Graeanog, Gwynedd. *Archaeologia Cambrensis*.

Evans, Jeremy forthcoming e. The Pottery from Bryn Eryr, Anglesey. In David Longley (ed.), Report on Excavations at Bryn Eryr. *Archaeologia Cambrensis*.

Evans, Jeremy forthcoming f. The Ewan Rigg Pottery. In Robert Bewley (ed.), Report on Excavations at Ewan Rigg, Cumbria.

Evans, Jeremy in prep. Function and Finewares; Some Trends in Romano-British Ceramics. *Journal of Roman Pottery Studies.*

Evans, Jeremy and Martin Millett 1992. Residuality Revisited. *Oxford Journal of Archaeology* 11(2):225-240.

Fowler, Peter J., R. S. Gardner and Philip Rahtz 1970. *Cadbury Congresbury, Somerset 1968: an Introductory Report.* Bristol.

Fulford, Michael G. 1975. *New Forest Roman Pottery.* Oxford: British Archaeological Reports (British Series 17).

Fulford, Michael G. and Karen Huddlestone 1991. *The Current State of Romano-British Pottery Studies: a Review for English Heritage.* London: English Heritage (occasional paper 1).

Gaffney, Vince and Martin Tingle 1989. *The Maddle Farm Project: an Integrated Survey of Prehistoric and Roman Landscapes on the Berkshire Downs.* Oxford: British Archaeological Reports (British Series 200).

Gidney, Louisa J. 1986. The Pottery. In Ken Fairless and Dennis Coggins (eds), Excavations at the Early Settlement Site of Forcegarth Pasture South, 1974-5. *Durham Arch. Journal* 2:34.

Gillam, John P. 1957. The Coarse Pottery. In E. J. W. Hilyard (ed.), Cataractonium, Fort and Town. *Yorkshire Archaeological Journal* 39:224-265.

Going, Christopher 1987. *The Mansio and Other Sites in the South-Eastern Sector of Caesaromagus; the Roman pottery.* London: Council for Brit. Archaeol.

Going, Christopher and Geoffrey Marsh forthcoming. The Pottery from Cefn Graeanog. In R. White (ed.), Report on Excavations at Cefn Graeanog, Gwynedd. *Archaeologia Cambrensis.*

Griffiths, Karen 1989. Marketing Roman pottery in Second Century Northamptonshire and the Milton Keynes Area. *Journal of Roman Pottery Studies* 2:67-76.

Hodder, Ian R. 1974. Some Marketing Models for Romano-British Coarse Pottery. *Britannia* 5:340-359.

Halstead, Paul, Ian R. Hodder and Glenis Jones 1978. Behavioural Archaeology and Refuse Patterns: a Case Study. *Norwegian Archaeological Review* 11:118-131.

Hill, Christopher 1980. *The Century of Revolution, 1603-1714.* 2nd ed. London.

Hingley, Richard 1989. *Rural Settlement in Roman Britain.* London: Seaby.

Kilbride-Jones, H. E. 1938. The Excavation of a Native Settlement at Milking Gap, High Shield, Northumberland. *Archaeologia Aeliana* (Ser. 4) 15: 303-350.

King, Anthony and Martin Millett forthcoming. The Samian. In P. John Casey, John L. Davies, and Jeremy Evans, *Excavations at Segontium 1975-79.* London: Council for British Archaeology.

Makepeace, G. A. 1983. A Romano-British Settlement at Staden near Buxton. *Derbyshire Arch. Journal* 103 (1984):75-86.

Marney, Pauline T. 1989. *Roman and Belgic Pottery from Excavations in Milton Keynes 1972-82.* Aylesbury: Bucks. Arch. Society (monograph 2).

Millett, Martin 1979. An Approach to the Functional Interpretation of Pottery. In Martin Millett (ed.), *Pottery and the Archaeologist*. London: London Institute of Archaeology (Occasional Publication No. 4).

Millett, Martin 1983. Excavations at Cowdrey's Down, Basingstoke 1978–81. *Archaeological Journal* 140:151–279.

Millett, Martin 1990. *The Romanization of Britain; an Essay in Archaeological Interpretation*. Cambridge: Cambridge University Press.

Millett, Martin and David Graham 1986. *Excavations on the Romano-British Small Town at Neatham, Hampshire 1969–79*. Winchester.

Mynard, Dennis (ed.) 1987. *Roman Milton Keynes: Excavations and Fieldwork 1971–82*. Aylesbury: Bucks. Arch. Society (monograph 1).

O'Leary, Timothy 1981. Excavations at Upper Borough Walls, Bath, 1980. *Medieval Archaeology* 25:1–30.

Pearce, B. 1942. Elizabethan Food Policy and the Armed Forces. *Economic History Review* (ser. 1) 12:39–46.

Pitt-Rivers, A. H. L. F. 1887. *Excavations at Cranbourne Chase*, vol. I. London.

Price, Jennifer 1989. Glass. In Mynard 1987, 147–157.

Redknap, Mark and Martin Millett 1980. Excavations on a Romano-British Farmstead at Elsted, West Sussex. *Sussex Arch Collections* 118:197–229.

Reece, Richard 1988. *My Roman Britain*. Cirencester.

Rivet, A. L. F and Colin Smith 1979. *The Place Names of Roman Britain*. London.

Selwood, Lynn 1984. Tribal Boundaries Viewed from the Perspective of the Numismatic Evidence. In Cunliffe and Miles 1984.

Silvester, R. J. 1981. An Excavation on the Post-Roman Site at Bantham, South Devon. *Devon Arch. Society Proceedings* 39:89–118.

Stead, Ian M. 1971. Beadlam Roman Villa: an Interim Report. *Yorkshire Archaeological Journal* 43:178–186.

Sunter, J. and Peter Woodward 1987. *Romano-British Industries in Purbeck*. Dorset Natural Hist. and Arch. Society (monograph no 6).

Thomas, Charles 1966. *Rural Settlement in Roman Britain*. London: Council for British Archaeology (Research Report 7).

Wainwright, Geoffrey 1990. *The Management of Archaeology Projects*. London: Historic Buildings and Monuments Commission for England.

Wainwright, Geoffrey 1991a. *The Management of Archaeology Projects* 2nd edn. London: Historic Buildings and Monuments Commission for England.

Wainwright, Geoffrey 1991b. *Exploring Our Past: Strategies for the Archaeology of England*. London: Historic Buildings and Monuments Commission for England.

Weatherill, Lorna 1988. *Consumer Behaviour and Material Culture in Britain 1660–1760*. London.

Young, Christopher J. 1980. *Guidelines for the Processing and Publication of Roman Pottery from Excavations*. London: D.A.M.H.B. (Occasional paper 4).

4

COLLAPSE THEORY
AND THE END OF BIRDOSWALD

Tony Wilmott

> We must accept that the soldiers of the Wall returned to the soil
> from which they sprang.

Thus, in the absence of evidence for the post-Roman period on the frontier, did Breeze and Dobson (1976: 232) conclude their account of Hadrian's Wall in the third and fourth centuries. Excavations by the Central Archaeological Service of English Heritage at Birdoswald, directed by the writer between 1987–92 have highlighted the period, and buildings post-dating the latest Roman coins and pottery have been recovered. Similar developments have also been found at South Shields, and in a more recent synthesis of Hadrian's Wall, Johnson (1989: 112) has cited these developments as the first real evidence that activity, of whatever kind, continued in the forts of the wall and its hinterland during the fifth century, suggesting further that as settlement nuclei, forts may have become local power centres with the potential to become 'part of the jigsaw that formed itself into the developing Northumbrian kingdom'. These discoveries alone, however, still lack a context as so little is known of northern Britain in the sub-Roman period. This paper constitutes a preliminary attempt to place the developments at Birdoswald into a somewhat more theoretical framework, and to provide some basis for future discussion.

Briefly, the Birdoswald evidence may be seen to reflect a transition from the 'Roman' occupation pattern of the late 4th century to a distinctive, and apparently 'non-Roman' pattern in the 5th or early 6th centuries. The evidence is located in the area immediately south of the *via principalis* of the fort, adjacent to the principal west gate. During the period from c. AD 200 to the 4th century this area was occupied by granaries of standard Roman military type. In the later 4th century, the raised and ventilated sub-floor of the southern granary was backfilled, and the flagstone floor relaid. A *terminus post quem* of AD 348 is provided for this by the latest coin in the backfill. At the western end of the building were a series of stone hearths, around which high quality finds were dropped. These included a glass finger ring and a gold earring; both mid-fourth century types, and also the latest coin from Birdoswald; a Theodosian issue dating to AD 388–395.

In the north granary the collapse of the roof after AD 353 was followed by the spoliation of the building for stone. It appears that the walls and the flagstone floor were extensively quarried. The former hollow sub-floor was now used for dumping. Pottery in the dumping suggests that it was contemporary with the reuse of the south granary. The coins are a better guide to date, however, and John Davies (forthcoming) has pointed out that the group of coins from this dump are later than those from the deliberate backfilling of the sub-floor of the south granary. The two groups are, in fact, complementary. The south granary backfill contained 23 coins of which the latest was dated to AD 348, and no fewer than fourteen ranged from AD 324–348. No FEL TEMP REPARATIO issues were present in this group. In the north granary dumping eight coins out of fifteen are dated to AD 348–378, beginning with FEL TEMP REPARATIO coins. Had later coins been circulating when the floor of the south granary was laid, there is little doubt that at least one would have been incorporated in the backfill. As this was not the case, the reflooring of this building cannot have been much later than c. AD 350. The dereliction and robbing of the northern building would have followed on closely after.

As well as the coins a pennanular brooch was found in the dumped material in the north granary. This was of a type identified by Margaret Snape (1992) as sub-Roman. An inscription commemorating the construction of a granary (RIB 1909) was found reused in the reflooring of an adjacent building during excavations in 1929 (Richmond and Birley 1930). The numismatic evidence confirms a *terminus post quem* after AD 364–375 for the phase during which the inscription was reused, based on a sealed coin of Valentinian I (ibid.: 174). The latest coin overlying this floor was dated by Kent (1951: 9) to after AD 389. It is entirely consistent with the evidence to suggest that the inscription was robbed from the north granary for immediate use in the building excavated in 1929.

Beyond the fact that they are stratigraphically later than the deposition of the coins and the brooch from the north granary, the following two phases cannot be dated. The first phase consisted of a group of two timber structures. One was built on the *intervallum* road of the fort to the south of the west gate. This was constructed using ground-fast posts, and utilised the west wall of the fort as one side. It was probably a lean-to construction. The main building was erected on the site of the north granary. The walls of the building were utilised as sleeper walls with post holes cut a single course deep into the wall tops. The floor of the building consisted of fissile micaceous shale flagstones which were laid over the earlier dumping and the collapsed roofing. Post holes were not found around the entire building, suggesting that elements of the stone walls survived to a higher level when the timber building was constructed.

The second phase, which was stratigraphically later than the phase of timber building just described consisted of a further group of buildings which appeared to be the functional successors of the first. Again buildings were erected on the *intervallum* road. This time, however, these were free-standing structures which did not utilise the Roman stone structure. The remains of the buildings were subtle, and difficult to recognise, as they were surface built using sleeper beams as footings, the imprint of which was barely discernible. The principal building was an altogether more impressive structure. Figure 4.1 shows site staff standing on the principal post-pads of the building, which measured 23.00m x 8.60m. It was defined by a row of stone post pads which ran parallel to the north wall of the former north granary, and by a shallow trench running the length of the former building. On examination, post pads corresponding to those in the northern row were found. The movement northwards of this building is probably significant. The north wall of the north granary (and therefore that of the first phase timber building) was built to respect the southern wall of the double-portal west gate. The south portal of the gate was blocked during the third century. The effect of this was to leave a band of dead ground amounting to half the width of the *via principalis* in front of the granary. The post-pad building was moved northwards to cover this ground, such that the north wall of the building lined up with the south side of the single portal gate. This careful consideration of the use of space within the fort, and the relationship between the building and the gate suggests that the building was of some status.

Sequences such as that found at Birdoswald are as yet rare in Britain.

Figure 4.1. Excavation staff mark out the principal post positions of the main building of the second phase of timber structures at Birdoswald (English Heritage).

The closest parallel is provided by Philip Barker's work at Wroxeter. Here the finds from the site were of late 4th rather than 5th century date, and a sequence of structural phases post-dating the appearance of the latest Roman material occurred. The re-flooring and partial demolition of the Basilica at Wroxeter is associated with coins of the House of Valentinian (Esmonde-Cleary 1989: 152; White 1990). The end of occupation is given a rough *terminus ante quem* by a carbon 14 date of ad 610±50 from a skeleton which was buried after the end of the timber building sequence (White 1990). In between these dates came successively a 'building yard' phase, the final demolition of the basilica, and the construction of a range of very substantial timber buildings on prepared platforms of rubble. The dating of the site is reliant on an assessment of the length of time buildings might have survived, or pathways been worn. the timber buildings at Wroxeter and Birdoswald were surface built on stone pads or reused walls, preventing the ground level rot which is a problem of ground-fast timbers. Properly maintained such a building could have lasted a very long time indeed. At Wroxeter, Barker (1985: 114) recognises the potential of such buildings to last anything from 25 years to a century, favouring a point midway between the two, and thus constructs a possible chronology for a sequence of three buildings. Barker (1985: 114–15; 1990b: 226) considers that the structural sequence is unlikely to have spanned less than one and a half centuries, and White (1990) sees the major timber building phase as lasting from AD 450–550.

Given the dating evidence at Birdoswald, alternative chronologies can be suggested. A minimum chronology for these phases would begin directly with the *terminus post quem* of AD 388–395 for the construction of the first timber phase, and would allocate 25 years life to each set of timber buildings, terminating the sequence c. AD 445. The maximum chronology would consider that the first timber phase, with its *terminus post quem* of AD 388–395 need not begin until AD 420. It may be even later if the reuse of the south granary was protracted, and the first of the large timber structures was its functional replacement. Adding a century for the lifetime of each of the two phases would provide a terminal date c. AD 620. An average may be taken assuming 50 years life for each timber building phase. This would mean that the post pad building would have been constructed c. AD 470, and the site abandoned c. AD 520. The writer is aware that both shorter and longer chronologies must, given the nature of the evidence, be considered valid.

The evidence for sub-Roman continuity at Birdoswald is substantial, as demonstrated by the above short summary. Though difficulties with chronology are at present insuperable, the transition from a the site as Roman fort to something which is different appears to the writer to be significant. The stages through which the site passes may have relevance to other sites where evidence for this period might be discovered. The stages may be categorised as phases of reuse and demolition, followed by adaptation, and finally rebuilding.

The first of these, a phase of reuse and demolition, is represented by the differing treatments of the two granaries during the mid-fourth century. The pattern at this time seems to be typical of one symptom of social and economic collapse described by Tainter (1988: 20), where:

> Little new construction [is undertaken], and that which is attempted concentrates on adapting existing buildings. Great rooms are subdivided, public space turned to private. When a building collapses the residents move to another.

The filling of the floors of the south granary suggest that the use of the building was changed. The domestic debris and hearths found within the building relate only to the final phases of its use, but suggest that this former 'official' building eventually acquired a private, domestic function. The north granary was quarried, and it seems likely that the building excavated in 1929 continued to be maintained as a 'rough shack' (Simpson and Richmond 1933: 262) using *spolia* from this building. Thus existing buildings were adapted and an official structure turned over to domestic use, while areas of the fort lay empty as buildings were quarried for materials.

A similar phase may also be represented by the 'building yard' phase at Wroxeter (White 1990: 5), and by the quarrying of road material at South Shields (Bidwell 1989: 89), if it is assumed that materials from the excavated areas of these sites were quarried for use elsewhere on these sites. A similar situation can be adduced at Exeter. Here, a new floor was laid in the basilica in or after the reign of Valens (AD 365–378). After the demolition of the basilica the products of demolition were removed wholesale, possibly for reuse elsewhere, before the area was given over to an organised cemetery by the mid-5th century (Bidwell 1979: 108–113).

There is no reason to suppose that the south granary could not have continued in use for a some considerable time. Greenhalgh (1989: 103) notes that the solid construction of civil *horrea* meant that they often survived to be reused with other functions. He cites those at Arezzo, used as housing by AD 876. In AD 895 the *horrea* at Trier, were reused as the '*monasterium s. Mariae vocatum Orrea*' (Eiden 1949: 73–74). Elsewhere (Wilmott 1988) it has been suggested that the granary was used as a hall. The evidence for this being the large hearths situated at one end of the building, and the fact that high quality finds were exclusively recovered from around these hearths.

The first large timber building falls technically and chronologically between the reuse of old buildings and the construction of new ones. It is not possible to be certain how much of the stone fabric was standing when the timber elements were constructed, but at least some parts of the building might have stood to some height, and that the building was partly stone and partly timber built. Buildings combining parts of ruinous stone structures with timber additions are known from at least three other sites. The latest phase of the south-west gate at South Shields included the replacement of the south-eastern arch with a timber gateway (Bidwell 1989: 89). At the temple of Uley, Gloucestershire, the collapse of part of the temple in the late 4th century was followed by the clearance of debris, and the modification and reuse of the surviving portions of the stone building, including an added timber framed element (Woodward 1993: 63–4). At Rivenhall

(Rodwell and Rodwell 1986: 63) a late or sub-Roman timber structure in the form of a projecting wing was added to the villa frontage, its construction similar to that of the fifth century Wroxeter buildings. The use of one earlier wall to build a lean-to structure, as appears to have been the case with the smaller building of the first timber phase is perhaps the easiest way of reusing existing fabric. This approach is exemplified in the fifth century Wroxeter complex (Barker 1981: fig. 5; White 1990: 6, fig. 13).

The final phase is one of rebuilding. The second timber building phase ignored the Roman stone structures and were constructed where required. The large building respected the west gate, and was clearly constructed with a spatial relationship with the gate as an important factor in its layout. The principal buildings of the timber phase at Wroxeter were similarly new constructions, taking no discernible pattern from their stone built forerunners.

The continuity of settlement attested stratigraphically appears, therefore, to be echoed in a gradual change in the way the inhabitants of the fort change the way in which space and existing building fabric is used. There is a logical succession of phases, from reuse to adaptation and then to rebuilding on new lines with different materials; a sequence which fits in well with the processes of building decay, and allows for habitation and decay to continue side by side. We have been fortunate at Birdoswald in being able to follow these processes within a clear stratified sequence, but they are stages which we should be looking for at every opportunity.

Who was doing all this adaptation and reuse? The obvious answer is that it was a result of continuity of settlement, and the lack of any archaeological hiatus confirms this. At Vindolanda Bidwell (1985: 46) has demonstrated that a refurbishment of the defences took place during the late 4th or early 5th century, and tenuously suggests that this could be seen in context with the refortification of western Iron Age hillforts in the 5th-6th centuries. This seems highly likely. The idea that the northern forts persisted as the sub-Roman defensive sites of the north is one which is emerging from work at Birdoswald, South Shields, and at Binchester. It is not, however a new idea; a Nennian reference which can be shown to refer to the fort at Old Carlisle encouraged Eric Birley (1951: 39) to 'suspect that it survived for many a long year after the "departure of the Romans" as a centre of sub-Roman civilization in Cumbria'.

This would fit with the documentary evidence for the survival of attenuated *romanitas* in the north and west within a series of small territories and kingdoms. In his report on the late 4th or 5th century refortification of Vindolanda Paul Bidwell (1985: 46) has tenuously suggested that this can

be seen in context with the refortification of south-western hill forts in the
5th and 6th centuries.

The radical changes in the type of settlement at Birdoswald at the end of
the fourth century and beyond are, of course, symptomatic of the more
general collapse of Roman Britain and the western empire at large. The
western Roman collapse has traditionally been regarded as an unparalleled
catastrophe, after which 'a period of recrudescent barbarism' (Wheeler
1932, on Lydney) set in, during which the inhabitants of the area 'sank
lower and lower in the scale of civilization' (Collingwood 1924, on
Cumbria). Tainter's (1988) recent examination of the phenomenon of the
collapse of complex societies cites Rome among a large number of
examples in which collapse can be seen as the result of declining marginal
returns on investment in complex social and political systems.

In the case of the Roman collapse, as summarised by Tainter (ibid.: 128–
52, 188, 196), the snowballing consequences of increased taxation on a
smaller and less productive population created apathy about the continu-
ance of Roman rule. Millet (1990: 212–30), summarising this period in
Britain, has suggested that the provincial elite took upon itself the deliberate rejection of centralised Roman government in AD 409, attributing the
revolt to 'those paying taxes for a defence and administration which no
longer served their needs' (ibid.: 228). Tainter (1988: 121) would rightly see
this as a decision deliberately to reject complex structures which have out-
lived their usefulness and thus to release resources to create a more
dynamic society, better able to cope with the stresses imposed upon it. The
phenomenon of collapse is seen, therefore, as part of a continuum; 'not a
fall to some primordial chaos, but a return to the normal human condition
of lower complexity' (ibid.: 198). While considering these ideas in the
winter of 1991/2, only a few months before this conference, it was illumin-
ating to watch the swift unfolding of an apparently similar process in the
former Soviet Union. Historians of the future will doubtless tell us whether
the events leading to the change of flag on the Moscow Kremlin in Decem-
ber 1991 can be seen in these terms, but at present they appear to inform
the problem. It seems arguable that the Soviet system was dismantled from
within at least in part as a result of the perception that investment in the
governmental structures of the union no longer served those paying for it.
The resulting dissolution of the union into its constituent republics was
almost universally welcomed as a result. To look at the period after the
Romano-British collapse in a non-pejorative manner must aid the understanding of that period as one not of catastrophe but of change, and change

which may to a great extent have been welcomed by many of those who participated in it, who could not know what result their actions might have.

By the third century at the latest, Britain was supplying the normal needs of the auxiliary units in the island, and this was formalised as late as AD 313 by legal hereditary service (Dobson and Mann 1973: 201). As late as AD 372 the sons of soldiers drew rations (Tainter 1988: 144). The direct result of a taxation revolt would be that the troops on the wall would no longer have been paid or supplied. Holder (1982: 103) compares Britain to other provinces where no combined effort was made against invaders by populations or garrisons, concluding that 'with no concerted effort in time of trouble individual units would have been destroyed . . . [or] faded away over a period of time' (ibid.). Esmonde-Cleary (1989: 142) cites the account in the *Vita Sancti Severini* of the *limitanei* of Noricum Ripense in AD 452. Pay had ceased, troops sent to get pay had been killed by barbarians, and consequently only a few very small formations were left. He suggests the same pattern for the British northern frontier.

A different model is suggested by the Birdoswald evidence. In the British diocese at large, Millett (1990: 218–19) demonstrates how the burden of the documentary sources shows *romanitas* surviving in the north and west in the second half of the fifth century in 'a series of different territories no longer knitted into the single whole which had existed before the expulsion of the imperial administration in AD 409' (ibid.: 218). Tainter (1988: 19) argues that when social organisation reduces to the lowest economically viable level 'groups which had been economic and political partners may become strangers or threatening competitors'. Given that the revolt of AD 409 would have thrown the wall garrisons, which by this time were probably not very large, onto their own resources, it is possible to visualise a pseudo-military structure remaining in place for some time. However it is also easy to see how a small cohort of *limitanei* might mutate into the *comitatus* of a leader, or succession thereof. The military and organisational partnership on the wall might break up, and only suitably positioned forts continue in occupation.

The material evidence for such a mutation might well take the form of the Birdoswald sequence. In each phase a long rectangular building appears to be the focus around which other buildings are constructed. In the final phase the importance of this building is stressed by significantly altering its position with relation to the fort gate. It is possible that these buildings were successive halls; central foci of a settlement type whose ancestry lies in the pre-Roman Iron Age, and in the less romanised area north of the Roman frontier rather than in the history and installations of the frontier itself.

This paper should be regarded as a series of interim statements and ideas based on work in progress. A number of themes appear to be emerging from the continuing analysis of the Birdoswald sequence, although these cannot as yet be placed into a coherent framework.

References

Barker, Philip 1985. Aspects of the Topography of Wroxeter, Viroconium Cornoviorum. In Grew and Hobley (eds) 1985, 109–217.

Barker, Philip (ed.) 1990a. *From Roman Viroconium to Medieval Wroxeter: Recent work on the Roman city of Wroxeter.* Worcester.

Barker, Philip 1990b. Open Area Excavation, Illustrated by the Excavation of the Baths Basilica at Wroxeter Roman City, Shropshire, England. In P. Francovich and D. Manacorda (eds), *Lo Scavo Archeologico: Dalla Diagnosi All'Edizione*, 205–234. Firenze.

Bidwell, P. T. 1979. *The Legionary Bath-House and Basilica and Forum at Exeter.* Exeter: (Exeter Archaeol. Reports 1).

Bidwell, P. T. 1985. *The Roman Fort of Vindolanda.* London: Historic Buildings and Monuments Commission for England (Archaeological Reports, 1).

Birley, Eric 1951. The Roman Fort and Settlement at Old Carlisle. *Transactions of the Cumberland Westmorland Antiq. Archaeol. Society* (new ser.) 51:16–39.

Casey, P. John forthcoming. The End of Garrisons on Hadrian's Wall: an Historico-Environmental Model.

Collingwood, Robin G. 1924. The Last Years of Roman Cumberland. *Transactions of the Cumberland Westmorland Antiq. Archaeol. Society* (new ser.) 24:247–255.

Davies, J. A. forthcoming. The Coins. In Wilmott, forthcoming.

Dobson, Brian and J. C. Mann 1973. The Roman Army in Britain and Britons in the Roman Army. *Britannia* 4:191–205.

Eiden, Hans 1949. Untersuchungen an den spatromischen Horrea von St Irminen in Trier. *Trierer Zeitschrift* (1949):73–98.

Esmonde-Cleary, A. S. 1989. *The Ending of Roman Britain.* London.

Greenhalgh, Michael 1989. *The Survival of Roman Antiquities in the Middle Ages.* London.

Grew, F. and B. Hobley (eds), 1985. *Roman Urban Topography in Britain and the Western Empire.* London: Council for British Archaeology (Research Report 59).

Holder, P. A. 1982. *The Roman Army in Britain.* London.

Johnson, S. 1989. *Hadrian's Wall*. London.

Kent, J. P. C. 1951. Coin Evidence and the Evacuation of Hadrian's Wall. *Transactions of the Cumberland Westmorland Antiq. Archaeol. Society* (new ser.) 51:4–15.

Millett, Martin 1990. *The Romanisation of Britain*. Cambridge: Cambridge University Press.

Richmond, Ian A. and Eric B. Birley 1930. Excavations on Hadrian's Wall in the Birdoswald-Pike Hill Sector, 1929. *Transactions of the Cumberland Westmorland Antiq. Archaeol. Society* (new ser.) 30:169–205.

Rodwell, W. J. and K. A. 1985. Rivenhall: Investigations of a Villa, Church and Village, 1950–1977. London: Council for British Archaeology (Research Report 55, Chelmsford Archaeological Trust Report 4).

Simpson, F. G. and Ian A. Richmond 1933. 1. Birdoswald, in Report of the Cumberland Excavation Committee for 1932; Excavations on Hadrian's Wall. *Transactions of the Cumberland Westmorland Antiq. Archaeol. Society* (new ser.) 33:246–262.

Snape, M. E. 1992. Sub-Roman Brooches on the Northern Frontier. *Archaeologia Aeliana* (5 ser.) 20:158–160.

Tainter, J. A. 1988. *The Collapse of Complex Societies*. Cambridge: Cambridge University Press.

Wheeler, R. E. Mortimer and Tessa V. Wheeler 1932. *Report on the Excavation of the Prehistoric, Roman and Post-Roman Site in Lydney Park, Gloucestershire*. London: Society of Antiquaries London (Research Report 9).

White, R. 1990. Excavations on the Site of the Baths Basilica. In Barker 1990a, 3–8.

Wilmott, Tony 1989. Birdoswald: Dark Age Halls in a Roman fort? *Current Archaeology* 116:288–291.

Wilmott, Tony forthcoming. Birdoswald on Hadrian's Wall: Excavations 1987–92. English Heritage (Archaeological Reports).

Woodward, A. 1993. The Uley Shrines. London: English Heritage (Archaeological Reports 17).

5

ANALYSIS OF SOCIAL AND CULTURAL DIVERSITY ON RURAL BURIAL SITES IN NORTH-EASTERN RAETIA

Manuela Struck

North-eastern Raetia differs from the rest of the province (west of the river Lech) in several respects: firstly, it was only conquered by the Romans during the Claudian – early Flavian period, and not under Augustus (Glüsing 1965: 7–8). Secondly, there are only few roads, namely a road along the south of the Danube, a north – south connection between Castra Regina (Regensburg) and Pons Aeni (Pfaffenhofen), and a road along the valley of the Isar heading for the Danube (Christlein 1977: 33; fig. 1). Thirdly, until now there is no indication for the existence of any *civitas* in north-eastern Raetia (Fischer 1990: 112). Fourthly, the archaeological material shows links to the adjacent province Noricum and to Germania.

It meant a drastic change to this – from a Roman point of view – underdeveloped part of the province, when in AD 179/180 the Legio III Italica was stationed at Castra Regina. This date is of great importance for the history of the region and the chronology of the sites.

As in the whole of Raetia our knowledge of Roman cemeteries from the middle Roman period in the north-east is still poor (cf. Kellner 1971: 124–25; von Schnurbein 1977; Mackensen 1978; Rieckhoff-Pauli 1979; Fasold 1985; Fasold and Hüssen 1985; Fischer 1985; Fischer 1990; Fasold 1992: 83). Research has been restricted to two regions: the neighbourhood of Regensburg (Fischer 1990) (Fig. 5.1) and the Isar valley (Struck forthcoming) (Fig. 5.2). Most of the cemeteries are completely or almost completely

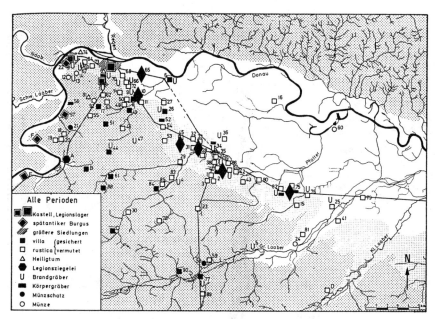

Figure 5.1. The region of Regensburg in the Roman period (after Fischer 1990).
Rhombuses mark the cemeteries discussed in this paper.

destroyed or only partly known. Planned excavations have only been undertaken very rarely. In two instances whole cemeteries have been excavated, namely the unpublished site of Mintraching (Lkr. Regensburg) and Ergolding (Lkr. Landshut) (Fig. 5.2 no. 15; Struck forthcoming). The latter contains 79 certain burials in an area of 73 m by 22 m and seems to have been used from the middle of the 2nd until the middle of the 3rd century (Fig. 5.3). Altogether there are 35 rural burial sites which all belong to *villae rusticae*. In addition to the 79 graves from Ergolding there are a further 78 from 12 other sites, which have only been partly uncovered, mostly in the course of rescue excavations. These graves date to the period from AD 80 to 260. Finally we have two small groups of burials which are known completely: Günzenhausen with 11 cremations from c. AD 130 to 170 (Fasold 1988) and the mausoleum of Niedererlbach within a walled enclosure (Christlein and Weber 1981; Kohnke and Struck 1985) (Fig. 5.4). Its seven graves – five in the building itself, two in the precinct – probably do not date before AD 180. Because of the described state of research Ergolding will stand in the centre of this article and results gained there will later be compared with the other sites.

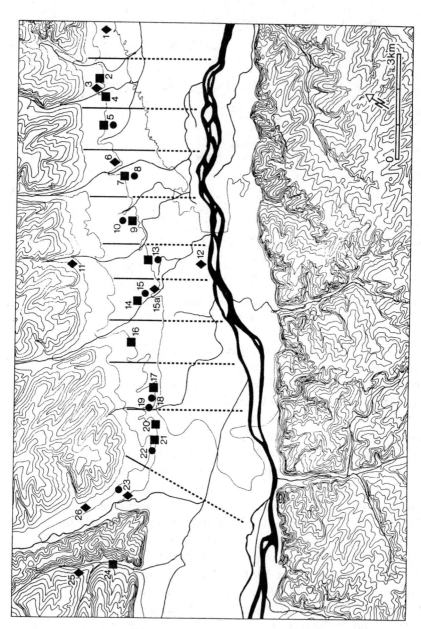

Figure 5.2. The lower Isar valley in the 1st to 3rd century AD with the estimated extent of the villa estates. Squares: villae rusticae; Dots: burials; and Rhombuses: finds of uncertain character (J. Koschorreck, Bayerisches Landesamt für Denkmalpflege, Landshut).

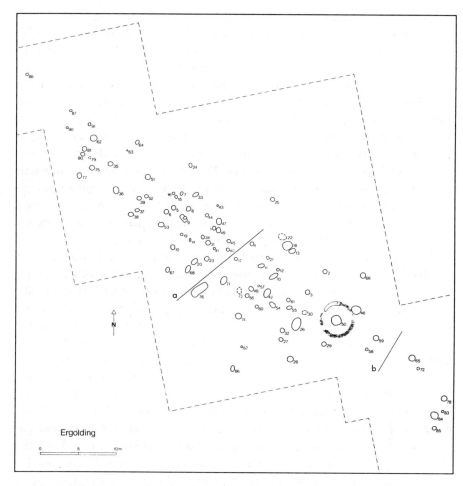

*Figure 5.3. The cremation cemetery of Ergolding, Lkr. Landshut (Lower Bavaria)
(after Christlein 1981: 36).*

Except for four inhumations from the first half of the 4th century
(Fischer 1990: 95) all the burials are cremations not later than AD 260. The
invasions of the Germans in AD 259/260 cause a break in the history of
north-eastern Raetia and therefore form the upper chronological limit of
this paper (Fischer 1990: 116–18).

In what follows the burial rite and archaeological material will be analysed to demonstrate the social and cultural diversity in this region. Evidence from settlements will be used in addition to the data from the cemeteries, but for our purpose the burials in this region offer the best data.

Apart from some neonates and small babies people were cremated. One finds the usual cremation types encountered in the rest of the empire in the middle Roman period. Characteristic for Raetia is the dominance of cremations with some sort of container for the cremated bone (Raetian burial custom described by Kellner 1971: 120 ff.; von Schnurbein 1982: 6–7; Fasold 1992: 11–19). But incinerations without urns are also found, so-called *Brandgrubengräber* (cf. Bechert 1980). Only in two instances had the dead been burned and buried on the same spot, in a *bustum* according to antique terminology (ibid.). As in the rest of the province the grave-goods had normally been placed on the pyre. Except for the urns there are only few unburnt objects in the graves. The inventories consist mainly of pottery which, together with the remnants of the pyre (charcoal, iron nails etc.), filled the simple grave pits of round or oval shape. Apart from some exceptions to be presented later no grave markers are preserved.

The population of north-eastern Raetia was seemingly well integrated in the distribution system of Roman objects, given the existence of glass, terra sigillata and other industrially manufactured pottery as well as items like bronze vessels, lamps, coins, *strigiles* and writing equipment. *Strigiles* and writing equipment also prove that the Roman way of life had been adopted to a certain extent as classical services of terra sigillata and mortaria demonstrate the knowledge of mediterranean cuisine and 'table manners'.

Nevertheless indications for a Romanised form of burial rite are rare: coins, lamps, incense burners, *unguentaria* and unburnt vessels for libations, as found in the graves of Rome and middle Italy (cf. Fasold 1993), do not appear very often and only on a few sites. Generally the Romanisation does not go far enough to suppress grave furnishing completely. With the exception of grave no. 26, only the mausoleum of Niedererlbach contains five cremations which bear all the signs of an Italic or Romanised burial rite: no grave-goods or hardly any secondary grave-goods (an unburnt lamp in one case is the only exception). In view of the monumental form of the funerary building, the glass urns and the quality of the few cremated objects, this lack of grave-goods does not document the low economic status of the buried, but a deliberately chosen kind of burial rite. Furthermore the whole floor of the mausoleum was covered with broken pottery which also filled a pit in the building (Kohnke and Struck 1985: 145–46). This seems to be the remains of a funerary feast or commemoration known from the written sources (Toynbee 1971: 50–51).

When we try to detect foreign elements in the burial rites of Raetia we have to consider the fact that we know hardly anything about native burial

C(ENTVRIAE) PAVLI.

Among the personal ornaments there is a quantity of so-called *militaria*, namely belt fittings (*cingula*) and fibulae typical for Roman soldiers. For example a fibula in shape of a horse (cf. Jobst 1975: 114) comes from the same grave as the graffito GENIO C PAVLI. Generally most fibulae have their main distribution in the noric-pannonian region (Struck 1992: fig. 4). From Flavian times onwards a resemblance in costume between Raetia and Noricum is no longer apparent (von Schnurbein 1982: 21). Nevertheless according to S. Riekhoff-Pauli Raetia still belonged to the so-called Danubian group of fibulae (Rieckhoff-Pauli 1975: 45). It is therefore not possible to prove an immigration from the east into north-eastern Raetia, but it seems highly probable. In the lower Isar valley two Iron knee-shaped fibulae have been discovered which very likely come from Germania (Fasold 1988: 183, 196 fig. 5, 4; Struck 1992: fig. 4, 6). In this context it should be mentioned that hand-made pottery of pre-Roman tradition constantly occurs in the material of the sites. The geological analysis of some pots shows that they are partly locally made and partly come from Germania (Fasold 1988: 214-15). So far it can neither be decided who made the pots in north-eastern Raetia nor how they came into this region. Immigration and trade are equally probable.

As there are good reasons to think the supply system and after-life belief were more or less uniform for the members of the community of Ergolding the quality – not quantity – of grave-goods, and the effort undertaken in building the grave can be taken as an indicator for the economic situation of the deceased or of the people who conducted the funeral. The qualitative classification of the grave inventories led to the recognition of seven groups which reach from 'rich' to 'poor':

I. elaborate grave construction, valuable 'antiques', precious metals and glass (with one exception not represented in the 3rd century);
II. large set of terra sigillata, glass and sometimes bronze;
III. small set of terra sigillata and glass;
IV. small set of terra sigillata or presence of terra sigillata, sometimes personal ornaments of bronze or iron;
V. fine ware (no terra sigillata) and glass;
VI. fine ware;
VII. only coarse wares.

The interpretation of these groups should not be taken too far, as such artificial constructs only serve as an aid for analysis. Nevertheless it is clear

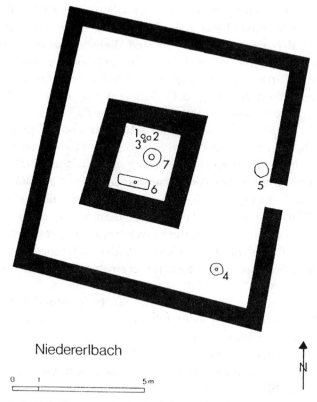

Niedererlbach

0   1   5 m

N

Figure 5.4. The mausoleum of Niedererlbach, Gde. Buch am Erlbach, Lkr. Landshut (Lower Bavaria) (after Christlein and Weber 1981).

that in the cemetery of Ergolding the whole population of a villa rustica is represented – both the owners and the workers (cf. van Doorselaer 1967: 24). Cemeteries of workers have for example been excavated at Courroux (Switzerland) and perhaps at Köln-Müngersdorf (Martin-Kilcher 1976: 102; Fremersdorf 1933: 85).

Regarding the distribution of grave-goods, burial rites and quality groups within the cemetery of Ergolding, two main parts can be identified on the plan: firstly, a central part with evidence for a Romanised burial rite and only few animal bones (meaning either no meat at all or more expensive bone-less pieces), with personal ornaments and a dominance of the higher quality groups (Fig. 5.3, mainly between line a and b). Secondly, a part north west of the central part with hardly any indications for a Romanised after-life belief, obligatory animal bones in the graves, only few personal ornaments, lower quality groups and a concentration of the hand-made pottery mentioned above. I was able to show that these distributions have no chronological relevance and interpreted them as the expression of at least two groups of people, different in culture and social status.

Turning to the other sites, we find a clear difference and spatial distinction at Niedererlbach too (Fig. 5.4). Whereas the Italic kind of burial practice was stressed above for the five cremations within the mausoleum, the two graves in the enclosure contain a large amount of primary gravegoods and pyre remains (Kohnke and Struck 1985: 145–46), as was customary in this province. Differences are not only to be found within the burial sites, but also when the single cemeteries are compared. At Günzenhausen for example the links to the east, with eastern pottery, fibulae and knives (Fasold 1988: 191–92) seem to be stronger than at any other site in the region and, as mentioned above, the graves from Niedererlbach show the highest degree of Romanisation. There are also differences between the sites concerning the care with which the cremated bone was selected, or the choice of pottery etc.

What was assumed for Ergolding above can be repeated for the other cemeteries: the archaeological evidence speaks for a heterogeneous population. This is well confirmed by the results gained from other Raetian sites – like Kempten-Cambodunum where M. Mackensen could detect a mixed population from Italy, the western provinces, Noricum, Germania and the Alps (Mackensen 1978: 181). In north east Raetia the connections to the east seem to dominate instead. Immigration is also attested by the epigraphical sources: K. Dietz for instance found evidence for the settlement of veterans from the Dacian wars under Trajan (Dietz 1984: 214) and for immigrants coming from the European provinces reaching from Hispania to Illyricum (Dietz and Weber 1982: 430 fig. 3). The archaeological traces of the pre-Roman inhabitants of Raetia north of the Alps are scarce (Schön 1986: 62 ff.). This can only partly be explained by the state of research: obviously the population was not large (Fischer 1990: 23–24). An organised settlement programme was necessary, reflected for example in the regular settlement pattern in the lower Isar valley (Fig. 5.2). Finally the stationing of the Legio III Italica was the moment when a large number of *villae rusticae* became necessary for supplying the troops. Thus the archaeological material of most settlements begins only in the the second half of the 2nd century (Fischer 1990: 115 fig. 'Karte 4'; Struck 1992: fig. 5). The gradual standardisation of the burial rites could then be understood as an expression of a mixed population growing together.

References

Bechert, Tilmann 1980. Zur Terminologie provinzialrömischer Brandgräber. *Archäologisches Korrespondenzblatt* 10:253–258.

Bittel, Kurt, Wolfgang Kimmig and Siegwalt Schieck (eds) 1981. *Die Kelten in Baden-Württemberg.* Stuttgart: Theiss.

Christlein, Rainer 1977. Die römische Isartalstraße von Moos-Burgstall bis Landshut. *Verhandlungen des Historischen Vereins Niederbayern* 103:30–50.

Christlein, Rainer 1981. Ausgrabungen 1980 und die Schwerpunkte archäologischer Forschung in Bayern. *Das archäologische Jahr in Bayern 1980:* 15–37.

Christlein, Rainer and Gerhard Weber 1981. Ein römisches Mausoleum bei Niedererlbach, Gem. Buch am Erlbach, Lkr. Landshut, Niederbayern. *Das archäologisches Jahr Bayern 1980:* 140–141.

Dietz, Karlheinz 1984. Das älteste Militärdiplom für die Provinz Pannonia Superior. *Bericht der Römisch-Germanischen Kommission* 65:159–268.

Dietz, Karlheinz and Gerhard Weber 1982. Fremde in Rätien. *Chiron* 12: 409–443.

van Doorselaer, André 1967. *Les nécropoles d'époque romaine en Gaule septentrionale.* Brugge: De Temple.

Fasold, Peter 1985. Totenbrauchtum im Voralpenland. In *Die Römer in Schwaben,* 186–190. München: Verlag Karl M. Lipp.

Fasold, Peter 1988. Eine römische Grabgruppe auf dem Fuchsberg bei Günzenhausen, Gem. Eching, Lkr. Freising (with a contribution by W. Polz). *Berichte der Bayerischen Bodendenkmalpflege* 28/29:181–215.

Fasold, Peter 1992. *Römischer Grabbrauch in Süddeutschland.* (Schriften des Limesmuseums Aalen Nr. 46).

Fasold, Peter 1993. Romanisierung und Grabbrauch: Überlegungen zum frührömischen Totenkult in Rätien. In M. Struck (ed.), *Römerzeitliche Gräber als Quellen zu Religion, Bevölkerungsstruktur und Sozialgeschichte. Internationale Fachkonferenz vom 18. – 20. Februar 1991 im Institut für Vor- und Frühgeschichte der Johannes Gutenberg-Universität Mainz,* 381–395. Mainz: Johannes Gutenberg-Universität Mainz.

Fasold, Peter and Claus-Michael Hüssen 1985. Römische Grabfunde aus dem östlichen Gräberfeld Faimingen-Phoebiana, Lkr. Dillingen a. d. Donau. *Bayerische Vorgeschichtsblätter* 50:287–340.

Fischer, Thomas 1985. Ein neues mittelkaiserzeitliches Brandgräberfeld aus Künzing, Lkr. Deggendorf. *Archäologische Denkmalpflege in Niederbayern* 26:174–178. München: Verlag Karl M. Lipp.

Fischer, Thomas 1990. *Das Umland des römischen Regensburg.* München: Beck.

Fremersdorf, Fritz 1933. Der römische Gutshof Köln-Müngersdorf. Berlin/Leipzig: de Gruyter.

Glüsing, Peter 1965. Frühe Germanen südlich der Donau. *Offa* 21/22:7–20.

Haffner, Alfred et al. 1989. *Gräber – Spiegel des Lebens. Zum Totenbrauchtum der Kelten und Römer am Beispiel des Treverer-Gräberfeldes Wederath-Belginum.* Mainz: Philipp von Zabern.

Jobst, Werner 1975. *Die römischen Fibeln aus Lauriacum*. Linz: Oberösterreichisches Landesmuseum.

Kellner, Hans-Jörg 1971. *Die Römer in Bayern*. 2nd ed. München: Süddeutscher Verlag.

Kohnke, Hans-Georg and Manuela Struck 1985. Archäologische Ausgrabungen in Niedererlbach, Gde. Buch a. Erlbach, Lkr. Landshut, 1980–1983 (with a contribution by M. Struck). *Archäologische Denkmalpflege in Niederbayern* 26:143–155. München: Verlag Karl M. Lipp.

Mackensen, Michael 1978. *Das römische Gräberfeld auf der Keckwiese in Kempten*. Kallmünz/Opf: Lassleben.

Martin-Kilcher, Stefanie 1976. *Das römische Gräberfeld von Courroux im Berner Jura*. Derendingen/Solothurn: Habegger.

Nuber, Hans Ulrich and Aladar Radnóti 1969. Römische Brand- und Körpergräber aus Wehringen, Lkr. Schwabmünchen. *Jahresberichte der Bayerischen Bodendenkmalpflege* 10:27–49.

Rieckhoff-Pauli, Sabine 1975. Münzen und Fibeln aus dem Vicus des Kastells Hüfingen (Schwarzwald-Baar-Kreis). *Saalburg-Jahrbuch* 32:5–104.

Rieckhoff-Pauli, Sabine 1979. Römische Siedlungs- und Grabfunde aus Künzing, Lkr. Deggendorf (Niederbayern). *Bayerische Vorgeschichtsblätter* 44:79–122.

Röring, Christoph Wilhelm 1983. *Untersuchungen zu römischen Reisewagen*. Koblenz: Numismatischer Verlag.

von Schnurbein, Siegmar 1977. *Das römische Gräberfeld von Regensburg*. Kallmünz/Opf: Lassleben.

von Schnurbein, Siegmar 1982. Die kulturgeschichtliche Stellung des nördlichen Rätien. *Bericht der Römisch-Germanischen Kommission* 63:5–16.

Schön, Franz 1986. *Der Beginn der römischen Herrschaft in Rätien*. Sigmaringen: Thorbecke.

Struck, Manuela 1992. Römerzeitliche Siedlungen und Bestattungsplätze im Unteren Isartal. Zur Besiedlung Nordosträtiens. *Archäologisches Korrespondenzblatt* 22:243–254.

Struck, Manuela 1993. Busta in Britannien und ihre Verbindungen zum Kontinent. Allgemeine Überlegungen zur Herleitung der Bestattungssitte. In M. Struck (ed.), *Römerzeitliche Gräber als Quellen zu Religion, Bevölkerungsstruktur und Sozialgeschichte. Internationale Fachkonferenz vom 18. – 20. Februar 1991 im Institut für Vor- und Frühgeschichte der Johannes Gutenberg-Universität Mainz*, 81–94. Mainz: Johannes Gutenberg-Universität Mainz.

Struck, Manuela forthcoming (1995). *Römerzeitliche Bestattungsplätze und Siedlungen im unteren Isartal*. Kallmünz/Opf: Lassleben.

Toynbee, Jocelyn M. C. 1971. *Death and Burial in the Roman World*. London: Thames and Hudson.

Urban, Otto H. 1984. *Das Gräberfeld von Kapfenstein (Steiermark) und die römischen Hügelgräber in Österreich*. München: Beck.

6

Locational Models and the Study of Romano-British Small Towns

Simon Clarke

Urban Hierarchies in Roman Britain ⎯⎯⎯⎯

When we attempt to consider the role played by urban settlements in Roman Britain we usually work on the assumption that larger settlements occupied a more senior position within the central place hierarchy. Hence a large city like Corinium is usually seen as having served as a major economic as well as administrative and political central place. Small towns like Worcester, which were clearly major centres for industry are often assumed to have performed administrative duties, as capitals of tribal septs or in some cases to have achieved *civitas* capital status. However it is clearly dangerous to assume that central place functions existed just because a large population is present. Clearly all men are not equal in the Roman world, in political terms for example one noble man is more significant than any number of landless farmers. When we consider the role that a settlement played we must remember that size is not important, its what you do with it that counts. This paper will reconsider the nature of the central place hierarchies in Roman Britain placing much more emphasis on the settlement's character rather than simply its size.

Christaller's Central Place Theory ⎯⎯⎯⎯

Central place analysis in archaeology has borrowed heavily from the New Geography of the 1960s. The most influential theory to be pressed into

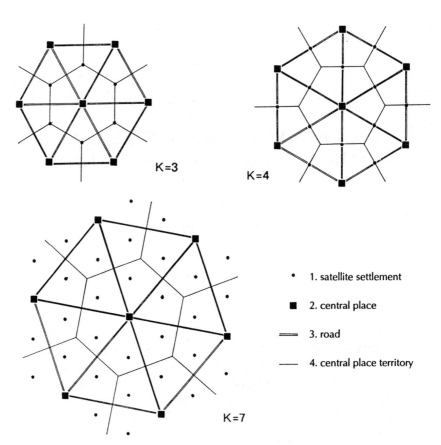

Figure 6.1. Christaller's central place theory.

service in the prehistoric and early historic periods is without doubt Christaller's model which attempts to define an optimal, least cost organisational structure within a network of related sites (Fig. 6.1). This was first outlined in the 1930s (Christaller 1935), but did not become widely known until it was brought to the attention of the English speaking world by Baskin in the mid 1960s (Baskin 1966). The theory is summarised by the following five points:

i. Specialisation. Even in simple agrarian societies, certain sections of the population demand products or services that they cannot provide for themselves. Service centres are necessary for the circulation and exchange of these services or products.

ii. Minimisation. To reduce the effort of obtaining services to a minimum they are agglomerated within a single centre, which is located centrally within a roughly circular territory. This also has the effect of maximising the trade opportunities for those offering the services.

iii. Lattice packing theory. Assuming a featureless plain with even population density a triangular arrangement of centres each surrounded by an hexagonal tributary area, has the most efficient geometric characteristics (Haggett 1965: 49).

iv. Tiered hierarchy. The settlement hierarchy would be made up of distinct levels.

v. Variations of the pattern. Within the above frame work a number of different patterns are possible. The three simplest hierarchies are as follows.

K=3, Market maximising hierarchy, secondary settlements lie at the boundary between three central places, to maximise choice of market. A settlement system based on this pattern is part of a highly commercialised society.

K=4, Transport maximising hierarchy, secondary settlements lie on roads between the central places. This too is a highly commercialised system.

K=7, Administrative hierarchy, secondary settlement lie entirely within the territory of the central place so that there is no scope for competitive marketing.

(Note that K refers to the number of settlements that lie within a central place field. Where a settlement lies on a boundary between central places it counts only as a fraction.)

APPLICATION OF THE CENTRAL PLACE MODEL TO ROMAN BRITAIN ⸺

Surprisingly little work has been directed towards locational models in the study of Romano British settlement since Ian Hodder's study of larger walled small towns (Hodder 1972) (Figs 6.2 and 6.3). Hodder saw urban location as conforming closely to Christaller's K=4 model. The model had much to commend it. That the large public towns were central places for the wider tribal area cannot be disputed. The choice of small towns plotted as the next layer in the hierarchy also appears logical as they do represent the largest walled areas. However there is no clear division in size or characteristics between second and third tiers of settlements as suggested

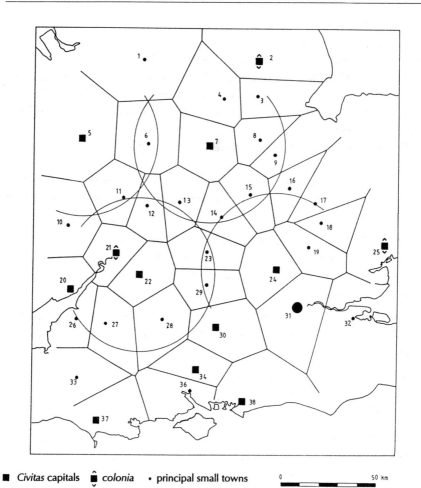

■ *Civitas* capitals ![colonia symbol] *colonia* • principal small towns   0   50 km

Figure 6.2. Small towns (after Hodder).

by Hodder. A number of walled small towns only slightly smaller than those towns plotted by Hodder might reasonably be added to the map, seriously disrupting his neat pattern of central places surrounded by six satellites.

GENERAL OBJECTIONS TO CHRISTALLER'S CENTRAL PLACE THEORY

One of the strongest objections to this use of central place theory is that there is a tendency to assume that lower order settlements develop chronologically after and at the dictate of the larger settlements. For instance Got-

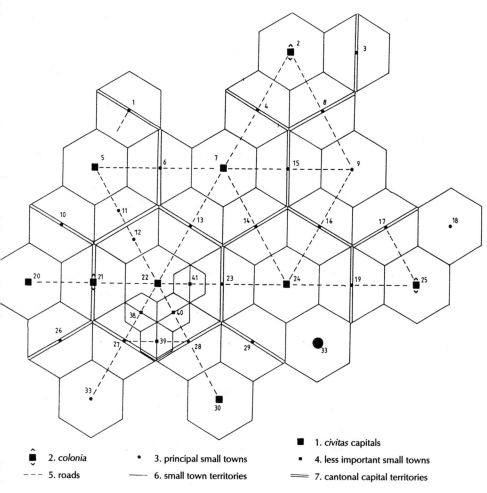

Figure 6.3. Schematic model of small town distribution in Roman Britain (after Hodder).

lund's model (Gotlund 1956), as utilised by Hodder, which suggested that secondary centres had developed at the intersection of two central place territories, where commercial competition was weakest. However Marshall argued that normally lower tiers of settlement hierarchy should come into existence before central places. Higher order settlements should develop as a result of stimulation from the preceding tier, not vica versa (Marshall 1964). In studies of Roman Britain this tendency has been encouraged by the obvious desire to work from known to unknown; from the better understood *civitas* capitals, to smaller urban sites, not all of which have been identified and which are generally much less extensively excavated.

A second and more fundamental objection to the application of Christaller's model to Roman Britain was its assumption that all central place functions were concentrated in a single location. The principle of minimisation of effort by agglomeration of functions at a single site cannot be taken for granted. The large numbers of major religious central places (for example Chedworth and Lydney Park) and production centres (for example the highly dispersed Oxfordshire pottery industry) located within the country side strongly suggest that centrifugal as well as centripetal forces were in existence. Furthermore there is a growing realisation that urban settlements did not take administrative responsibility proportional to their importance as commercial centres. Conversely industry did not necessarily take off at the important administrative and cultural centres. Corinium though a *civitas* and possibly later a provincial capital has so far produced very little evidence for industrial production. Sjoberg has noted that societies' administrative elite and merchant and artisan classes were drawn to the same locations by their mutual interdependence. Merchants and artisans needed a market for their goods while the aristocracy needed the material symbols of power and to keep a tight grip on what was an alternative power base, which might have become a threat to their traditional position (Sjoberg 1960). However there is some reason to believe that these elements in society repelled as well as attracted each other. Although this is a factor which has frequently been overlooked it should come as no shock to the student of urbanism. It has long been noted that towns, while acting as centres dedicated to the perpetuation of the ruling class and their value system (Sjoberg 1960) on one hand, also acted as a source of innovation, social change and modernity on the other. Of course what one element of society saw as progress could be seen by another as social pathology, moral disorder and destruction of the community (Holton 1986: 1). Although the landed elite needed the services of merchants and artisans they might have wanted to limit their contact with such a polluting influence. Artisans and merchants might similarly have withdrawn from those elements of society which sought to depreciate manual and commercial activity as degrading. In short the models proposed by Christaller and used by Hodder were two simplistic. The relationship between settlements cannot be treated as a single dominant force. It must be broken down into its constituent parts: political, military, ideological and economic.

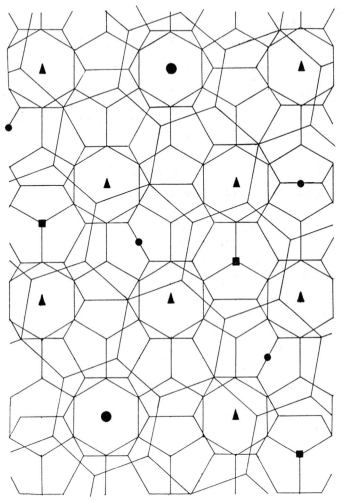

● Acts as a central place in the K=3, 4 and 7 systems   ■ Acts as a central place in the K=4 and 7 systems
● Acts as a central place in the K=3 and 7 systems   ▲ Acts as a central place in the K=3 and 4 systems
   note that only sites that act as central places to more than one system have been plotted

Figure 6.4. Losch's modification to central place theory.

LOSCH'S MODIFICATION ————

Christaller's model assumed fixed-K hierarchies in which the relationship
between settlements at one level could also be applied to higher levels.
Christaller himself noted that under ideal conditions administrative, trans-

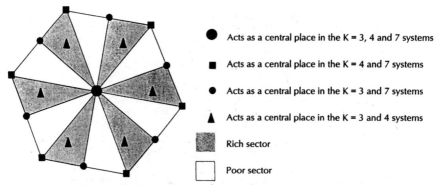

Figure 6.5. Rich and poor sectors in the Loschian landscape.

port and market central place systems had different requirements. A modification to the model was proposed by Losch in which the requirement that central place functions be concentrated in a single location was removed allowing the K=3, 4, 7 and higher order systems to diverge in their selection of central place locations (Losch 1954) (Fig. 6.4).

If the different order hierarchies are rotated about a common hub until the maximum number of central places overlie each other a predictable pattern emerges. Figure 4 demonstrates the principle with just K=3, 4 and 7. The Loschian landscape created by the overlaying of many hierarchies (the nine simplest K systems) with a city centre at the hub, was one of twelve alternating rich and poor sectors (Haggett 1965: 122, 124, figure 5.9) in other words, sectors which contained many central places and those with relatively few (see Figure 6.5).

The theory has been used to explain rich and poor city sectors in modern cities, including Chicago (Haggett 1983: 391), but its relevance here is in explaining the distribution of minor urban sites around the *colonia* and *civitas* capitals of Roman Britain. For the sake of simplicity the landscape has not been built up past the K=7 hierarchy. As a result a pattern of contiguous hexagons has been created. This consists of a single settlement which operated as a central place to all three hierarchy systems and eighteen settlements which possessed various combinations of two central place functions (see Figure 6.6).

VARIATIONS IN THE SMALL TOWNS ———

In the Roman period these 'two function' central places might have been represented by the so called small towns. This settlement class was perhaps

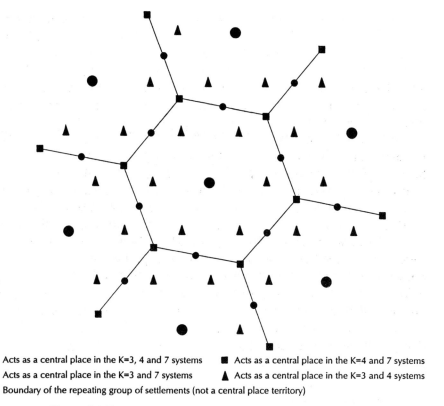

● Acts as a central place in the K=3, 4 and 7 systems   ■ Acts as a central place in the K=4 and 7 systems
● Acts as a central place in the K=3 and 7 systems   ▲ Acts as a central place in the K=3 and 4 systems
—— Boundary of the repeating group of settlements (not a central place territory)

Figure 6.6. Repeating pattern of multiple function central places.

the most heterogeneous that has been applied to Roman Britain. Some possessed populations that were as large as those in the smaller *colonia* and *civitas* capitals, defensive circuits and large scale industry. The prime example of such a site was Water Newton. Others were without defences and would be better thought of as villages or 'local centres' as Hingley (1989) has described them. The Losch modification to Christaller's central place model may therefore be useful, not in its predicative ability, which Hodder thought so helpful (Hodder 1972: 887), but in helping to explain the variety of forms which urbanism could take.

THE EMERGENCE OF *CIVITAS* CAPITALS ————

It is important to stress that the settlement which is central to the hexagon in figure 6.6 is not a higher order central place serving the surrounding settlements. However it is unique amongst the settlements of its hexagon in bringing all the central place functions together to one location. With this advantage that site might be the obvious choice as central place should a higher tier develop in the settlement hierarchy. This might explain why some Iron Age central places develop into urban centres in the Roman period, while others do not. In the Dobunni region there are at least four sites which have some claim to be oppida, but only one of these, Bagendon seems to have become fully urban, being succeeded by Cirencester a short distance away. The other sites were not wholly abandoned as central places however. Minchinhampton oppidum was succeeded by the major villa at nearby Woodchester (Clarke 1982), while another oppidum, Grim's Ditch became the location of a group of major villas. Such sites are frequently overlooked as central places even though Woodchester in particular is built on a scale similar to that of the largest public buildings. Villas of this order were certainly the homes of important 'central people' and as such occupy positions at the centre of extensive patronage systems. Similarly the large hillfort or oppidum at Salmonsbury (Bourton-on-the-Water) took on some but not all major central place roles in the Roman period. It became a communications node and important commercial centre, but failed to develop an important cultural or administrative role, although it may have been the site of a mansio.

CONCLUSION

In conclusion it can be said that a *civitas* region closely resembled a net-work of central places on the model of Losch rather than Christaller. The city represented the hub of the system, upon which all central place fields, from the highest to the lowest order focused. This created a fully urban site with a large non-agricultural population, planned form, defences and legal autonomy. The settlements of the *civitas* hinterland however presented a contrasting picture. Central place fields were out of phase due to the varia-tions in their sizes. A number of central place functions could gather together in a single location by chance, but never with the frequency that they did at the systems hub, the *civitas* capital. This led to the creation of a range of rural and only semi-urban centres, some of which are commonly called small towns. Losch's work has often been overlooked as too complex a model to transfer from the uniform plain to the highly variable landscape of the real world. However I am not suggesting that his model can explain the distribution of central places so much as their character. *Civitas* capitals were all pretty much of a much, their form easily described. Characterising small towns has proved much more difficult, requiring almost as many categories as known examples. I believe Losch's model helps us to understand this diversity and explains why there can never be a satisfactory definition for the minimum requirements of an urban site.

References

Baskin, C. W. 1966. *Central Places in Southern Germany.* New Jersey.

Christaller, W. 1935. *Die Zentral Orte in Suddeutschland.* Jena.

Clarke, Giles 1982. The Roman Villa at Woodchester. *Britannia* 13:197–228.

Haggett, P. 1983. *Geography: a Modern Synthesis.* 3rd edition. Cambridge.

Godlund, S. 1956. *The Function and Growth of Bus Traffic within the Spheres of Urban Influence.*

Haggett, P. 1965. *Locational Analysis in Human Geography.* London.

Hingley, Richard 1989. *Rural Settlement in Roman Britain.* London: Seaby.

Hodder, Ian R. 1972. Locational Models and the Study of Romano-British Settlement. In David L. Clarke (ed.), *Models in Archaeology,* 887–909. London.

Holton, H. J. 1986. *Cities, Capitalism and Civilization.* Boston.

Losch, A. 1954. *The Economics of Location.* New Haven, Connecticut: Yale University Press.

Marshall, J. V. 1964. Model and Reality in Central Place Studies. *Professional Geographer* 16:5–8.

Sjoberg, G. 1960. *The Pre-Industrial City.* New York.

7

PROLOGUE TO A STUDY OF ROMAN URBAN FORM

Simon P. Ellis

The archetypal Roman town was not the kind of urban form to which we could easily relate today. Its monotonous rectangular street grid seems unfocused and cold, like the lay out of many modern American cities. This paper is intended as a first step in applying the ideas of modern town planning to Roman cities. By studying the Roman city with the eyes of those who seek to create urban forms it may be possible to address a question that the Roman archaeologists have increasingly posed themselves in moments of self-doubt. Was the Roman town a functioning community, or was it an artificial product born out of the Roman mania for organising everything?

In considering the modern town the planner looks for certain facilities. These can be classified as buildings for community use, shopping centers, housing, industry, and transport infrastructure. I see no reason why we should not look at Roman towns the same way. Some of these topics may seem inappropriate in studying Roman towns. On the other hand we all must approach history with our modern preconceptions, and in adopting an approach based on modern town planning my prejudices at least may be more explicit.

Since the theories of modern town planning have hardly ever been used in archaeology there are an enormous number of lines of enquiry to pursue. Moreover to fully resolve many of the points I have raised would require an exhaustive consideration of ancient texts. This paper can thus only be seen as a prologue to the study of Roman urban form.

First I wish to explore the street grid. Roman cities can be divided into two groups of forms; the 'planned' and the 'unplanned'. By 'planned' I do not mean those that were pre-meditated, but rather those whose urban design was made to follow a specific regular urban design. 'Planned' cities range from new settlements like the relatively small Republican colonies of northern Italy, to a large capital city like Carthage, which continued to expand using a regular street grid of equal size *insulae* from the first century BC to the fifth century AD. 'Unplanned' cities, may have expanded following general principals of development laid down by the authorities, but they do not have such a regular urban design. They tend to be pre-Roman settlements, or those that grew up spontaneously at river crossings, road junctions etc. In these the earlier settlement controls the form of the later one, and the significance of a road or river crossing dominates the future pattern of growth.

This distinction between 'planned and unplanned' is preferable to the traditional assumption. This sees Roman urbanism as the Roman Republican colony and its strictly rectangular street grid. Following the republican period it is then assumed that 'true orthogonal planning dwindled as erratic street patterns appeared ever more frequently' (Macdonald 1986: 25). This theory does not account for cities such as Carthage where new suburbs continued to follow the Augustan street grid and *insula* until at least the early fifth century AD (fig. 7.1). Nor does it account for the continual construction of new formally planned towns throughout the Roman period, including for example Caricin Grad in the sixth century AD.

The ideal Roman 'planned' town does not seem to have been designed for ease of 'navigation'. Whilst a rectangular street grid does lend itself to easy directions of the 'four blocks forward and one to the right' type, it does not provide direct routes from point A to point B, as anyone finding their way around a North American city knows. Although it was theoretically easy to find one's way to the forum, or capitol, by following the Decumanus Maximus, or Cardo Maximus, traveling to any other point in a regular Roman city was difficult. Macdonald (1986: 32–33) considered the streets of a Roman city as 'connective architecture' or 'continuous conduits', in which the architecture of the street facades provided 'few abrupt changes of formal ambiance once the main gate has been passed'.

A number of planning theorists have stressed the importance of street design in finding one's way through a city. In the 1950s Lynch (1960) studied the mental maps of local inhabitants. He found that there were five types of significant feature – landmarks, nodes (major junctions of confluences of traffic), paths (major roads), edges (the borders of familiar street

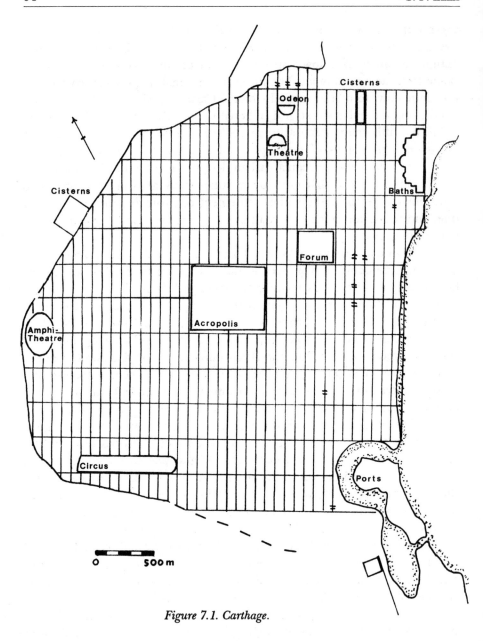

Figure 7.1. Carthage.

facades), and districts (neighbourhoods with a very strong character).
When locals were asked for directions these features were mentioned
rather than other less recognisable elements of the city architecture. The

degree to which a city was made up of these distinctive architectural elements made up its 'legibility'. A 'legible' city was one which had a strong distinctive character, to which its inhabitants could easily relate.

The description by Lynch (1960: 61) of the rectangular street grid of Los Angeles could be applied to many Roman towns:

> Almost every subject [questioned] could easily put down some twenty major paths in correct relation to each other. At the same time, this very regularity made it difficult for them to distinguish one path from another.

Recent work by Hillier (Hillier and Hanson 1984) has considered the way that streets, or 'paths' in Lynch's terms, penetrate districts. Hillier noted that legibility should be hierarchical. That it should be possible to distinguish a main through road, from a side road, and from a residential street. There was thus a hierarchy of roads. If it was not possible to distinguish between a main road and a side road then traffic tended to get lost in the side streets, or through traffic could end up in residential neighbourhoods. Main roads should be distinguishable by factors such as width, or lack of pedestrian access. In residential neighbourhoods the homes should open onto smaller streets, which should be narrower or winding to emphasise that they were not designed for traffic. Hence in modern estates red brick is used instead of tarmac, and flower boxes are placed in the road to slow cars down after the German style of 'traffic calming'.

In these circumstances it would have been easier to find the way across a small ancient town than a large modern city. On the other hand ancient Carthage consisted of some 200 regular *insulae*, and must have been confusing. Later in the sixth to seventh centuries AD many streets became blocked and impassable (fig. 7.1). Though this may have caused traffic problems it may have increased legibility, since only a few streets were now major cross-town routes.

Hillier and Hanson (1984) also introduced the concept of 'permeability', which indicates the degree to which streets enter an estate. They suggested that it should be difficult enough to find one's way into an estate, so discouraging intruders yet not too difficult for the residents to find their way out. Hence a modern estate has a complex network of access roads, but often includes some pedestrian short cuts to the shops.

Hillier (Hillier and Hanson 1984: 21–22) would regard the Roman town plan as one in which the global needs of society dominate the local needs of the settlement. 'The global system is defined only by the relations between

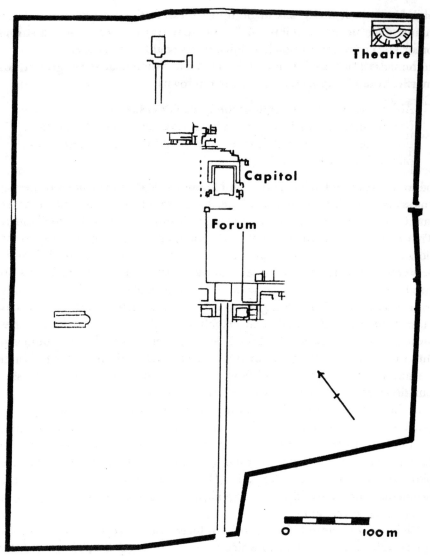

Figure 7.2. Luna (after Frova).

the major ceremonial buildings linked as they are by "causeways".' The local system is one like that of a medieval town, in which intricate street networks give full play to street life, and neighbourhood formation.

The relative uniformity of Roman street grids and frontages, discouraged 'legibility', and the formation of neighbourhoods. In Hillier's terms 'permeability' was too great since it was easy to travel right across the city on most roads. The Decumanus or Cardo Maximus might be somewhat larger than other streets, but otherwise there was little to distinguish the frontages, or colonnades. Instead the Roman would have had to use distinctive land-marks. In other words the principle was one of 'turn left after the Baths of Caracalla' rather than 'go down the street with all the bay windows'.

The lack of differentiation in the width of streets also suggests that the Romans were not much concerned with traffic flow. It is quite common for a wide main street of a Roman town to have steps across it. Provincial settlements grew up around clearly distinguishable major through routes between major towns, but in a planned town like the second century BC colony of Luna (Fig. 7.2), the Via Aemilia, one of the grandest routes of the empire, just looks like a rather wide street when it passes through the town. There is no indication of measures to deal with any resulting traffic conges-tion.

When spontaneous 'unplanned' settlements, such as many of the small rural towns of Roman Britain, grew up the settlement orientated itself towards the major road which is as a consequence clearly identifiable. Houses open onto the main thoroughfare: side streets are narrow and of lesser importance. These points can be illustrated by the plans of two important cities of the Roman period Ephesus and Dougga. Though both were founded in pre-Roman times they saw a considerable amount of re-building in Roman times.

EPHESUS (FIG. 7.3) ————

Ephesus was a great classical city with a long history. Although its plan was partly determined by two hills on the east of the site, it can in many ways be seen as a prototypical example of Greek and Roman urban design.

Foss (1978: 56–57) notes the difference between the two main late antique streets of Ephesus, the Arcadiane and the Embolos. The Arcadiane ran from the harbour to the centre of the town, at the theatre. At 10.7m in width plus colonnades on either side it was the grandest street in the town, yet to Foss it is 'cold and lifeless' compared to the Embolos. The Embolos was a narrower street that curved uphill from the theatre to the municipal buildings. It was lined with large numbers of statues. There were numerous late antique graffiti on the facades and the pavement.

Both streets were fronted by shops but as Foss concludes the Arcadiane 'was a monument and vital artery, but not a centre of urban life'. The nar-

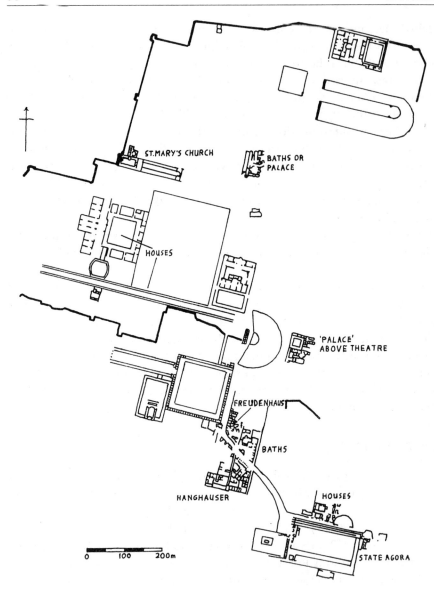

Figure 7.3. Plan of Ephesus (after Foss).

rower width and steep slope of the Embolos meant that it was less suited to wheeled, or four legged traffic. At the same time its position outside the municipal buildings lined with statues of past politicians made it an ideal centre for political discussion and abuse. In the case of the Arcadiane there seems to be a contradiction between its monumental aspect and its use as a 'main artery'. I am inclined to think that it was the monumental aspect that was most important, and that it was designed for ceremonial processions of dignitaries who had arrived by sea. Though its great width made it eminently suitable for wheeled traffic I think its ceremonial function was more important than its commercial one.

In Hillier's terms the Arcadiane was the 'causeway' built by the central administration to link the main public buildings. Although the Embolos was lined with statues of civic dignities it had a great deal of 'character'. This character was created by its lively street life, its narrow width and winding route, the statues along it, and a great variety of building facades (e.g. Temple of Hadrian). To Lynch it would be a very 'legible' street. The facades would create two clear edges to the districts on either side. To the west there were civic buildings set against the steep hill of the acropolis. To the east there were rich houses, set attractively on a gentler slope overlooking the street.

Dougga (Fig. 7.4) ⸻

By contrast to Ephesus, there is very little of the 'planned' in Dougga (Poinssot 1983). For much of its history Dougga remained part of the territory, or *pertica* of Carthage. There was a community of Roman citizens in the town from 46 BC, but the town did not gain full municipal status until AD 205.

Nevertheless it would be wrong to imagine that the city grew without guiding principles. It is commonly stated that the plan of Dougga derives from that of the earlier Numidian settlement. In truth there is little clear archaeological evidence for the plan of the Numidian settlement. Dougga is a typical hill top town and like such settlements all over the world, of all periods, its streets simply follow the topography of the ground.

Most of the public buildings in Dougga date from the later second century AD. Many (like the theatre, the Temple of Caelestis, and the Temple of Saturn) are sited to take advantage of views across the rich agricultural valley that provided the city's wealth. There were virtually no straight streets anywhere in the town. At first sight this would seem to make it very hard to find one's way across town, but I would suggest the opposite is true. Public buildings are spread evenly across the town, and wherever a pedestrian was there would always be one nearby. The public buildings would be useful landmarks in directing people. Their various

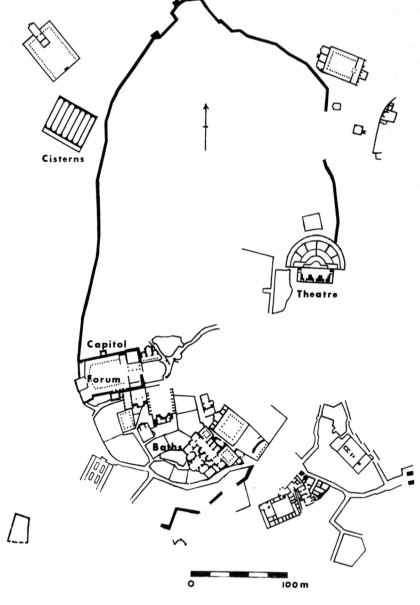

Figure 7.4. Plan of Dougga, Tunisia (after Poinssot).

facades, as at the Embolos in Ephesus, would combine with the winding routes of the streets to create a strong neighbourhood identity.

Dougga was thus a very 'legible', easily understood city. Town planners have found that people today generally prefer a town with strong character and 'legibility'. Given the choice between living in a planned Roman colony and Dougga I expect most people today would choose the latter.

In the law of 45 BC, the *Lex Heraclea* (*CIL* I: 593) Caesar decreed that after the tenth hour in the evening, only vehicles were allowed to travel the streets of Rome. The streets, he said, were too crowded with pedestrians in the day time, and only in this way could passage be secured for wheeled traffic (Carcopino 1940: 62–63). Nevertheless the law was not extended to the rest of the empire until the second century AD.

The impression is that Roman towns were not designed for wheeled or hoofed traffic. At both Ephesus and Dougga it is possible to find many streets which have steps across them or which are very narrow. Ease of access never appears to have been considered when locating important buildings. At Ephesus, it was the social context which determined the form of the streets rather than the need for access. If a visiting dignitary arrived at the city by sea expecting to give an important speech at the civic assembly, his triumphant procession up the Arcadiane would have been followed by a more ignominious climb up the narrower, steeper, bustling Embolos.

The Roman town was inturned and closed like the Roman house, which presented a blank exterior to the outside world (see further below). If, as I have been implying, it was often difficult to find one's way round a 'planned' Roman town then it is legitimate to ask who the towns were designed for. Did the Roman towns function more for residents or for outsiders and regular visitors? Residents would have been more familiar with the landmarks that would have been used for finding one's way according to Lynch's theory. Visitors may have found it very difficult, and the whole experience may have seemed rather daunting if they came from the countryside and had not seen cities before. Simon Clarke has shown in this volume how the location of Romano-British towns can be explained by an aim to obtain the best possible location for an administrative, or market centre. The arguments in his paper and mine bring out the use of towns to 'control' a society. This does not necessarily mean military or political control. It may rather be control over the movement of goods and people, guiding them along certain routes, which can be observed or from which they can be directed to certain key locations.

The tendency in the western provinces to place all the public buildings in a single central location, could be seen as an attempt to create legibility of the town plan. It can also be seen as a way of making sure that most visitors to the town are directed towards the political and economic centre of the settlement. Two major factors can be found to influence the location of major public buildings, politics, and available land, but not access.

In modern town planning preparing for major new developments, involves what is known as the 'land assemblage' problem. This involves buying up the plots of many smaller owners to assemble the site for a very large building. As more and more small owners sell up the developer becomes more and more financially committed to the project, because of the purchase of so much land, and pragmatically because he is increasingly the owner of a large part of the site. The last pieces of land to be bought, or 'assembled' are known as the 'ransom strip'. This is because the developer is so committed that he can be held to ransom by the last of the small owners who can demand an exorbitant price. If the developer does not pay, he is left owning three quarters of the land, but unable to build.

At Carthage it is notable that all the major public buildings of the second century AD – theatre, baths, circus, amphitheatre, lie outside the kernel of the ancient city. Recent excavations suggest that these major buildings were built at the edge of the urban area of that time. It is not possible to tell whether this was an attempt to avoid site assemblage problems, but it does indicate a desire, at the very least, to avoid the political problems of demolishing the property of, and dispossessing, a large number of citizens.

In Rome a more radical solution to the site assemblage problem, as suggested by ancient authors, was to start a fire in the area (Plutarch *Crassus* 2.5; Suetonius *Nero* 16). Though there could be large open areas in Roman towns these would still have been under private ownership and site assemblage problems would have resulted. Arson is said to have been a successful strategy as it made the price of the land crash.

The public baths is perhaps the institution of the Roman world which most closely resembled a modern community centre, and thus had the potential to 'control' the lives of the townspeople. In the Mediterranean there were normally several distributed throughout the town. Thus the Baths can be said to be a neighbourhood facility. On the other hand there were not really enough baths to cover every neighbourhood. Baths were normally financed by private munificence rather than by systematic state provision, and were maintained by an entrance charge (Juvenal *Satires* II). The impression is that people had their favourite baths and would travel across town to visit it. Perhaps the best analogy is the modern leisure centre, of which their can be two or three in larger towns located in 'main centres'. If we accept this view then it seems inescapable that in Roman Britain the systematic construction of public baths as part of the forum complex was a deliberate attempt to encourage Roman behavior in the natives, as Agricola is said to have intended (Tacitus *Agricola* 21). The Romans were deliberately using urban design to influence local people.

Some Roman cities had formal markets. Sometimes these were stalls in the forum. In other places for example at Wroxeter in Britain, there were purpose-built market buildings. However the majority of shops seem to have been spread throughout the town. In large Roman cities it is common to see shops flanking the entrances to the big houses. The shopkeepers were presumably tenants, and had the added advantage of providing more security to the big house.

Shop-keepers also found themselves under obligation to the community. In late antique Antioch shopkeepers were obliged to provide lamps to light the porticoes outside their premises (Amm Marc 14.1.9). Street lighting was also provided in late antique Alexandria and Constantinople, but not in early imperial Rome (Foss 1979: 56–57, Bean 1979: 140). In Romano-British towns, shop-keepers and traders often lived in the traditional 'strip houses' with a shop on the street, living quarters behind, and a yard, or workshop to the rear again. There is much debate amongst classical historians, as to whether trades were concentrated in particular streets or neighbourhoods (MacMullen 1974: 66–70). The evidence does not seem conclusive. Suffice to say there was no form of 'shopping centre', or anything to compare with the medieval 'souq'.

The Roman house has more in common with the modern oriental types of house than with those of present day Europe. The Roman house was in-turned as regards both its architecture and its life. It did not present many openings onto the street. There was often an entrance corridor, and reception suite, but these formed a part of the house. This is different to the 'intermediate zone' between house and street, that is formed by the modern front garden, or the verandah. This intermediate zone, studied by Glassie (1975: 137), and other analysts of urban form, creates an area, which is half in the house, and half in the street. Residents can feel they are still at home, passers-by can feel they are not intruding, and interaction can take place freely.

The shops and stalls in the colonnades of streets such as the Embolus at Ephesus, appear to create such an intermediate zone, but this is deceptive.

Most interaction with the Roman householder took place inside the house in an area clearly under the control of the owner (Wallace-Hadrill 1988; Ellis 1991). The fact that much of Roman political and economic negotiation took place behind closed doors helpd to explain the conspiratorial nature of Roman politics. Though many Roman cities, especially those in the Mediterranean clearly had a sense of 'community', at least as expressed in the munificence of their leading citizens, the closed nature of the Roman house did not allow for open socialising in a local neighbourhood.

The conclusion from this brief overview of planning in Roman towns is that, in terms of the overall plan, and in terms of the location of the main public buildings within that plan, the Roman town was an environment which exerted a large amount of control over its inhabitants movements. There is also evidence that control was exerted through particular types of buildings. Social pressure was placed on the inhabitants in the public baths, and the residences of the rich were used by their owners to enhance their power over others.

References

Bean, G. 1979. *Aegean Turkey*. London: Benn.

Carcopino, J. 1940. *Daily Life in Ancient Rome*. Harmondsworth: Penguin.

Ellis, Simon P. 1991. Power, Architecture and Decor: How the Late Roman Aristocrat Appeared to His Guests. In Gaza (ed.), *Roman Art in the Private Sphere*, 117–134. Ann Arbor: University of Michigan.

Foss, C. 1979. *Ephesus after Antiquity*. Cambridge: Cambridge University Press.

Glassie, Henry 1975. *Folk Housing in Middle Virginia*. University of Tennessee.

Hillier, Bill and Julienne Hanson 1984. *The Social Logic of Space*. Cambridge: Cambridge University Press.

Lynch, K. 1960. *The Image of a City*. Cambridge, Mass. Massachusetts Institute of Technology Press.

Macdonald, W. 1986. *The Arcitecture of the Roman Empire II: an Urban Appraisal*. New Haven: Yale University Press.

MacMullen, Ramsay 1974. *Roman Social Relations 50 BC to AD 284*. New Haven: Yale University Press.

Poinssot, C. 1983. *Les ruines de Dougga*. Tunis: I.N.A.A.

Wallace-Hadrill, Andrew 1988. The Social Structure of the Roman House. *Proceedings of the British School at Rome* 56:43–97.

8

SYMBOLS OF POWER AND NATURE: THE ORPHEUS MOSAICS OF FOURTH CENTURY BRITAIN AND THEIR ARCHITECTURAL CONTEXTS

Sarah Scott

INTRODUCTION ─────

The aim of this paper is to demonstrate the importance of studying mosaics within the social/architectural context. As Preston Blier (1987: 1) has pointed out, architecture is invariably anthropocentric, being bound up with human activity, experience, and expression. Mosaics, as integral features of architectural design, must also be seen as socially constructed. The approach to be employed here will involve the identification and location of those sites possessing Orpheus mosaics, and an analysis of the nature of representation. A part of this analysis will consider similar representations in other contexts and media, in order to provide new insight into the possible significance of Orpheus within fourth century Britain. The final part of the discussion will concentrate on the social/architectural contexts of the pavements, and an attempt will be made to explain the evidence in the light of this.

THE DATA ─────

Before carrying out any kind of analysis it is necessary to identify and locate representations of Orpheus on floor mosaics, and to place them within some kind of chronological framework. It will be useful to divide the

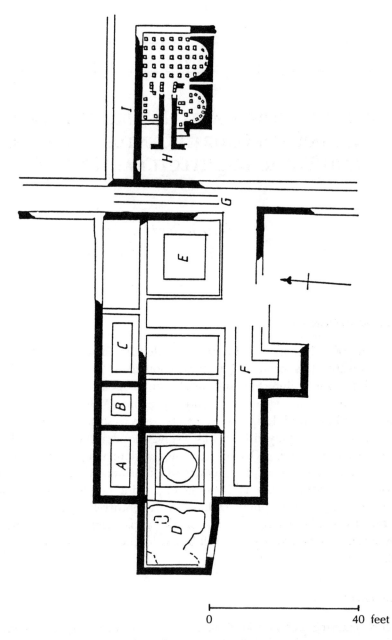

*Figure 8.1. Rooms with mosaics at Withington villa
(corresponding mosaics in Figure 8.2) (after Lysons 1817).*

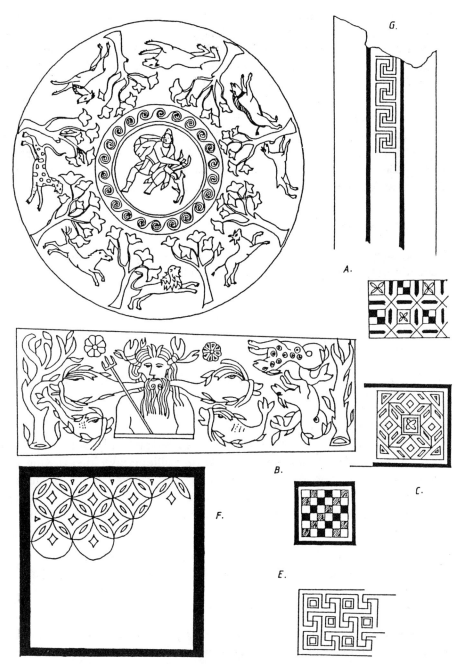

Figure 8.2. The mosaics at Withington villa (after Lysons 1817).

pavements into two groups: definite examples, and possible examples. Within the first category there are eight pavements: Barton Farm (Buckman and Newmarch 1850); Withington (Lysons 1817) (Figures 8.1 and 8.2); Woodchester (Lysons 1817); Newton St. Loe (Nichols 1838); Littlecote Park (Hoare 1819) (Figure 8.3); Winterton (Stead 1976) (Figure 8.4); Horkstow (Hinks 1933), and Brading (Price 1881) (Figure 8.5). Within the second category there are a further seven pavements: Dyer Street (Beecham 1886); Whatley;[1] Wellow;[2] Pit Meads (Hoare 1819); two pavements from Caerwent (Toynbee 1964: 266), and some fragments from Bishopstone.[3] The distribution of these pavements is summarised in Figure 8.6. The main aspects of the data are summarised in Figure 8.7.

REPRESENTATION ───────

In considering art forms in the archaeological record it is necessary to consider not only what is represented, but also how it is represented. As Boas notes (1955: 13):

> It is essential to bear in mind the twofold source of artistic effect, the one based on form alone, the other on idea associated with form. Otherwise the theory of art will be one-sided.

With regard to Romano-British Orpheus mosaics, it will be important to assess the 'meaning' of Orpheus in the light of classical mythology, while also paying attention to the formal relationships within the mosaics, and the effect of form on meaning.

In mythology, Orpheus was the greatest singer and musician conceived by the Greeks. He was the son of the Muse Calliope, by either a King of Thrace or Apollo. Apollo gave him a lute with which he was able to charm wild beasts and make rocks and trees move. Jesnick (1989: 10) has noted that the character of the Orpheus image is defined by its difference from other scenes in the animal genre:

> for the singer achieves by his art what otherwise takes great physical courage and skill. Men have only a tenuous hold over the captured beasts, who, always seeking to escape, eventually kill, or are killed. Orpheus stills this endless cycle.

The animals traditionally found on the Orpheus scene are those which exhibit types of behaviour which make them difficult to handle or capture. The animals represent both the negative and the bountiful aspects of

Figure 8.3. Mosaics at Littlecote Park (after Vertue 1730).

Figure 8.4. Mosaic at Winterton (after W. Fowler 1796).

nature, which Orpheus is able to control and hold in balance. The lion and the leopard are those animals most frequently represented in the Romano-British pavements, as is the case throughout the empire.

The majority of the Romano-British Orpheus mosaics employ the following scheme (Figure 8.8):

Orpheus is usually found at the centre of the pavement, surrounded by animals and birds. The central position of Orpheus emphasises his power, while the surrounding concentric circles reflect the nature of this power;

Figure 8.5. Mosaic at Brading (after Price 1881).

the animals are 'contained' by his charms. Another important feature of this design is that it can be viewed from any angle and still be understood. It is also possible to comprehend the central figure as someone possessing power without having to understand who he is, or the mythological background.

If we are to further understand the significance of Orpheus within Romano-British mosaics, it will be useful to assess the evidence for similar forms of representation in other contexts and media.

REPRESENTATIONS IN OTHER CONTEXTS

There are a number of representations in Britain which share physical attributes with Orpheus i.e. they are wearing similar clothing and are accompanied by animals. For example, at London (Merrifield 1986); Chedworth (Toynbee 1962: 156); Bisley (Clifford 1938); Upton St. Leonards (Rawes 1977); Box (Toynbee 1964: 179); Wilsford (Toynbee 1964: 179); Nettleton

(Wedlake 1982); Thruxton (Ingram 1849), and Lydney (Wheeler 1932). Three sculptures from London, termed 'hunter gods', of mid-fourth century date, are dressed in short tunics, a cap similar to that worn by Orpheus, and carry a short sword. At least two of the examples are accompanied by a dog and a deer. Merrifield (1986: 87) suggests that these figures probably came from a substantial Roman building which might have been a temple complex, the meeting place of a religious guild, or a residence with private shrines. Merrifield (ibid.: 89) proposes that these figures, and others with similar characteristics from the sites mentioned above, are the result of highly sophisticated and constructive religious thought. In support of such an argument are the parallels between the hunter god and Apollo and Orpheus. There is a relief from Ribchester, identified by its inscription as Apollo Maponus, in which the composite deity is represented with a quiver on his back, a lyre by his side, and apparently wearing a cap. It is likely that Apollo acquired this head-dress by a double association; with Orpheus through their common attribute, the lyre, and with Mithras through his solar connections (Merrifield ibid.). Hunter gods from the north and south-west have also been identified with Silvanus, god of the woodlands and wildlife.

To summarise, it seems that there was a cult figure in late Roman London, almost certainly under official patronage (ibid.: 87), who appears to be a conflation of Apollo, an oriental mystery god, and a native deity representing nature. It suggests someone in authority in London with a strong interest in comparative religion and the initiative to develop a new syncretic cult. This cult seems to have been popular in southern and central south-western England. Returning to the Orpheus mosaics, it can perhaps be suggested that his popularity, particularly in the central south-west, had something to do with his conflation with the hunter god identified above (Henig 1986: 17). In addition to the shared physical similarities, there are also the shared connections with power and nature.

It is interesting at this point to consider the interpretation of the Littlecote pavement proposed by Walters (1982). Walters has suggested that Orpheus acts as a link between Apollo, of whom he was a priest, and Dionysus, the principal deity of the cult alluded to in the mosaic. We are meant to see Apollo and his priest Orpheus. The same dual personality can be attributed to each of the four surrounding female figures. Walters (ibid.) suggests that the figures are semi-detached for reasons of allegorical narrative. They are seasons, but they are also goddesses representing the cycle of life, death, and resurrection. All of the animals, Dionysiac in form,

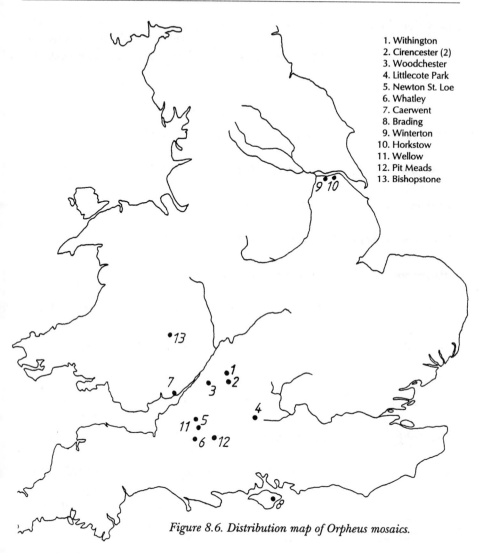

1. Withington
2. Cirencester (2)
3. Woodchester
4. Littlecote Park
5. Newton St. Loe
6. Whatley
7. Caerwent
8. Brading
9. Winterton
10. Horkstow
11. Wellow
12. Pit Meads
13. Bishopstone

Figure 8.6. Distribution map of Orpheus mosaics.

were also intended to convey the same theme.

In order to pursue these ideas further, the mosaics have to be placed within the social/architectural context of their construction and use.

THE HISTORICAL CONTEXT ———

The early fourth century saw a 'flowering' of villas in Britain, particularly in the south-west. A number of factors were responsible for this move to the

Table 8.1. Summary of the evidence for Romano-British Orpheus mosaics.

DEFINITE	Description	Date	Location
Barton Farm	Concentric circles	coins c.293 c.300-25	Reception area
Withington	Concentric circles	c.325-50	Reception area
Woodchester	Concentric circles	c.300-25	Reception area
Newton St. Loe	Concentric circles	c.325-50	Reception area
Littlecote Park	Radial (circular)	c.360	Reception area
Winterton	Radial (circular)	c.350	Reception area
Horkstow	Radial (circular)	c.350	Reception area
Brading	Medallion	4th century	Entrance hall
POSSIBLE			
Dyer Street	Concentric circles	4th century	Reception area?
Whatley	Square (concentric)	c.350-60	Reception area
Wellow	Uncertain	4th century	Reception area
Pit Meads	Circular (?)	4th century	Reception area
Caerwent (1)	Fragment	?	?
Caerwent (2)	Rectangular panels	?	?
Bishopstone	Fragments	4th century	?

countryside, one of the most important being the problem of inflation in the third century, and the debasement of the silver coinage from Caracalla onward. At this time the state preferred to collect taxes in kind, and the larger landowners were obviously the best equipped to deal with the

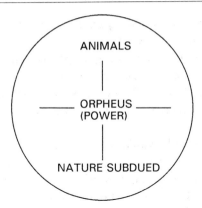

Figure 8.7. Orpheus representations schematically interpreted.

problem of taxation. As a result of this, a rigidly ordered society was being created, induced by the state's need to gather as much revenue as possible, and by the tendency of the territorial magnate to increase his estate by taking over the land of those who were not rich enough to survive in the changed world.

It is clear that, by the fourth century, the villas had become the primary centres for status display. As Millett (1990: 197) notes, those clients and others who required services from the powerful would come to them for an audience, and in all probability this would have been at their rural residences. The incentive for public display in the towns had disappeared by the early fourth century, and the later Romano-British villas should be seen as a re-direction of the surplusses of society towards personalised rather than communal display (ibid.).

Scott (1990: 169) has suggested that general trends in villa design, such as symmetrical facades, wings, courtyards, and enclosures, are related to the changing social situation noted above. She points out that these features first made their appearance in villa design in the second century, at about the same time as the establishment of a market economy, with the scale and degree of formalisation of these design elements reaching a peak in the fourth century. Scott (ibid.: 170) suggests that these architectural features express a duality of purpose. On the one hand they represent a sophisticated attempt at entry into the Romanised world of markets and 'civilisation', and on the other, they are an attempt to distance the household from an environment thought to be potentially hostile. This hostile environment was not just the perceived physical threat of barbarians. There was, Scott (ibid.) suggests, a more insidious threat: vulnerability to market forces and therefore poverty, inflation, taxation, and the need to accept strangers over the threshold.

An analysis of those villas possessing Orpheus mosaics can, I suggest, contribute a great deal to the argument outlined above. In particular, it will serve to highlight a number of changes that were taking place throughout the fourth century in terms of the manipulation of architecture within social relations.

Concerning the villas and mosaics constructed in the earlier part of the fourth century, it does seem that the sites fit in with Scott's argument. The architecture obviously aims to impress, while also allowing the villa owner to control access to and within his home. Woodchester (Figure 8.9), for example, possesses three courtyards, and symmetry was obviously a major consideration in its design (Clarke 1982). Clarke (ibid.) notes that the site of the villa rises slightly towards the inner courtyard and room 1, and these features must have formed a topographical and architectural climax. Additionally, room 1 was vast; nearly 50 ft. (15m) square, with its floor entirely covered with the Orpheus pavement. As to the superstructure, Clarke (ibid.) suggests that a domed roof would be consistent with the concentric design of the pavement and the presence of columns, but the walls seem insufficiently buttressed, especially to the south. Another possibility is that the columns supported a gallery, and if so, this would have enabled the pavement to have been appreciated to best advantage. As yet, however, there is no evidence for a staircase. Both of the possibilities outlined above would have enhanced the impact of the Orpheus pavement. An important point to note is that room 1 most probably had four entrances, one in the centre of each wall. It would almost certainly have been the first room that was entered by guests. I suggest, therefore, that it would probably have been used for reception purposes; a form of reception hall where the patron could meet his clients, and perhaps also the location for large scale banquets. On entering the corridor (room 2), the visitor would have been on a visual axis with room 1, with Orpheus, and possibly a central fountain,[4] in view. Once in the room, the visitor may have been able to view the other corridors leading away to further wealth and splendour. Those guests who were on a sufficiently intimate footing with the owner may have been invited to experience this wealth beyond. The 'depth' to which a guest was able to penetrate the building, and the route that he took, emphasised the nature of his relationship with the owner.

Ellis (1991: 127) has noted that in late antique houses, statues of gods and mythological heroes were often employed to glorify the owner. Mosaics

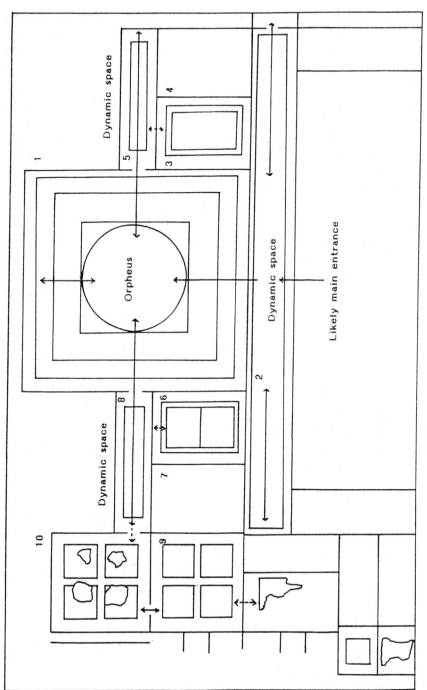

Figure 8.8. Viewing patterns at Woodchester villa.

were often used for the same purpose, for example, in North Africa many home owners commissioned pavements with hunt scenes, in which the owner himself was portrayed as the hero of the hunt. It is not unlikely that the owner of the villa at Woodchester chose Orpheus for similar reasons. Orpheus was able to control nature in its strongest and wildest forms without the use of physical force, and would therefore have been an appropriate choice for a room in which the owner would have conducted business, and entertained friends and/or strangers, and generally aimed to impress. The villa owner was associating himself with godly powers. As Ellis (1991: 126) notes, such interpretations might seem farfetched were it not for Ammianus's description of the flattering comparisons made to senators in Rome. Additionally, Diocletian attempted to raise the office of emperor to a transcendent plane, as did Constantius 2 in fourth century Rome (ibid.: 129). If the emperors could be seen as gods, then it is not unlikely that a villa owner could associate himself with a mythical hero.

It seems that other less wealthy villa owners in the area were sufficiently impressed by the Orpheus pavement at Woodchester to commission such pavements for themselves. Although they may not have possessed such considerable means, they certainly had similar ambitions and aspirations. Based on the chronology outlined in Table 8.1, it could be suggested that 'emulation' (Miller 1982) was taking place. The owner of the villa at Woodchester could be seen as a form of 'local emperor'. In order to improve their position within the social hierarchy, other villa owners in the area, at Barton Farm, Withington, and Newton St. Loe, for example, may have adopted this powerful symbol.

The villa at Littlecote represents, I think, a further development of these ideas. The room possessing the mosaic is, in fact, separate from the main villa building. It also lacks heating, and would probably have been cold and damp given its situation by a river. Walters (1982) has suggested that this hall would have been used for ceremonial purposes, perhaps the meetings of an unrecognised sect or fraternity in fourth century Britain. I would suggest, however, that this hall may instead have been a reception hall. Such chambers have been identified by Ellis (1988) in Roman and provincial houses, and they consist of large apsidal rooms, preceded by a vestibule, that can be entered through the main door of the house onto the street. The location of the halls next to the street would have ensured the maximum amount of privacy for the family. The aristocrat presumably appeared in the apse surrounded by his retainers (Ellis 1988: 569). Bek (1983: 91) has noted that in imperial palace architecture the apse was envisaged as a backdrop for the emperor. This idea of the apse as a backdrop for persons or events, rather than sculptures or furniture, may be relevant in the case of Littlecote. The 'hall' possesses both a vestibule and apses, and was also separate from the main villa building. It may have been here that the owner met his clients, perhaps appearing in the apse at the far end. The villa owner kept his public and private life separate, and perhaps only a privileged few would have been admitted to the main building. The mosaic itself, with its complex religious images, would have emphasised the formality of the architecture and the superiority of the villa owner. Those visitors who lacked the necessary education would have been excluded from the significance of the design, and their social distance from the villa owner would have been further emphasised.

It is interesting to note that the villas at Horkstow and Whatley have similar large halls, and both date to around the mid-fourth century, or slightly later. Like Littlecote, the Horkstow pavement is complex in its imagery, and combines Orpheus with a number of other mythological subjects.

These developments in domestic architecture coincide with the developments in religious thinking discussed briefly above. Looking back to the evidence for the 'hunter god', it is possible to suggest that the elite of mid-fourth century Britain felt it necessary to promote religious ideas in which various gods and deities were conflated, and in which the emphasis was on power over nature. This pattern fits in with changes that were occuring elsewhere in the empire. As Henig (1986: 194) suggests:

> we must not ignore the deepening religious response of the fourth century Roman (and provincial) aristocracies in the fourth century, pagan as well as Christian. For the emperor Julian, Homer, Vergil and other Greek and Roman authors were writers of 'holy writ'.

The pagan resistance was undoubtedly widespread, but its core in the west was the Roman senate which, after Rome had ceased to be the capital of the Roman empire, assumed once more in Roman history a conspicuous role (Bloch 1963: 194). Notable evidence for such a revival in Britain occurs in the form of the Mildenhall Treasure (Painter 1977) and the Corbridge Lanx (Haverfield 1914), both of which appear to date from around the reign of Julian (355–363), and whose pagan character can hardly be disputed. By commissioning pavements with complex pagan images, the owners of the villas at Littlecote and Horkstow may have been associating themselves with these religious elites elsewhere in the empire, while also asserting their own individuality through their inventive syncretism.

Ellis (1988: 573) proposes that the architectural developments may be associated with two historical trends: the concentration of wealth and power in the hands of a few aristocrats, and a change in the form of personal patronage. According to Sidonius (ibid.: 575), mid-fifth century Gaul appears to have been dominated by a villa-based aristocracy, with more autocratic relations between patron and client. The government was investing more power in local aristocrats, and in 371 landlords were made legally responsible for the collection of taxes. The only way that the poor could resist demands from officials and aristocrats was by resorting to someone with more power, even if they risked losing their liberty in the process (ibid.: 576). The construction of a hall such as that at Littlecote would have helped the villa owner to assert and maintain his authority. The patron could have appeared 'godlike' in the apse, surrounded by complex and impressive decor. The separation of the room from the main villa would have distanced the owner from the 'domestic' scene, stressing the contrast with those visitors whose main concern would have been domestic issues and survival in the changing world. The 'rules' that governed meetings between patron and client, and the repetition of such 'rituals', would have meant that these social relations were constantly reinforced through everyday actions.

CONCLUSIONS ————

In summary, it has been suggested that the Orpheus pavements of the first half of the fourth century represent overt statements of power on the part of the villa owners. The nature of the designs would probably have enabled visitors or residents of the villa, from all social backgrounds, to comprehend the central figure as a figure possessing power. The Orpheus pavements are commonly found in reception or dining rooms at this time, and would almost certainly have been the rooms seen first by guests. Guests may have obtained glimpses of the rooms beyond, and according to their degree of intimacy with the owner may have been invited 'deeper' within the villa. The divisions between the 'public' and 'private' areas of the villas seem to have become more clear cut after the mid fourth century. In some cases visitors may not have been allowed to penetrate the villa at all, and were received instead in a separate hall, or audience chamber. The power of the villa owners may have become more autocratic by this time, and the architecture would have removed them from the domestic setting into an almost religious context. The complexity of the designs would have emphasised the social differences between patron and client, and these differences would have been reaffirmed through the everyday use of the architecture.

One other point to note is that the villa owners themselves may have had apprehensions regarding their own security, both in this life and the next. The increasing concern with complex religious ideas may have been an attempt on their part not only to assert their superiority within the social order, but also to associate themselves with various deities and to obtain their protection. The conflation of numerous gods may have increased their feelings of security in a period when empire wide problems were making their future seem increasingly uncertain.

NOTES ————

1. V.C.H. Somerset 1, 1906, 317.
2. V.C.H. Somerset 1, 1906, 312–314.
3. B. Walters – Paper presented at the 25th Symposium on Roman Mosaics, 7th Dec. 1991.
4. Research carried out by the Woodward brothers for a reconstruction of the pavement suggested water staining around the centre of the pavement, which may have been caused by a fountain.

References

Beecham, K. J. 1886. *History of Cirencester and the Roman City of Corinium.* Cirencester.

Bek, L. 1983. Questiones Convivales: the Idea of the Triclinium and the Staging of Convivial Ceremony from Rome to Byzantium. *Analecta Romana* 12:81–107.

Bloch, H. 1963. The Pagan Revival in the West at the End of the Fourth Century. In A. Momigliano (ed.), *The Conflict between Paganism and Christianity in the Fourth Century,* 193–218. Oxford.

Boas, Franz 1955. *Primitive Art.* New York: Dover.

Brendel, O. J. 1979. *Prologemena to the Study of Roman Art.* New Have: Yale University Press.

Buckman, J. and C. H. Newmarch 1850. *The Remains of Roman Art in Cirencester.*

Clarke, G. N. 1982. The Roman Villa at Woodchester. *Britannia* 13:197–228.

Clifford, E. M. 1938. Roman Altars in Gloucestershire. *Transactions of the B.G.A. Society* 60:297–307.

Cookson, N. 1984. *Romano-British Mosaics.* Oxford: British Archaeological Reports (British Series 135).

Coward, R. and J. Ellis 1977. *Language and Materialism*. R.K.P.

Ellis, Simon P. 1988. The End of the Roman House. *American Journal of Archaeology* 92:565–576.

Ellis, Simon P. 1991. Power, Architecture, and Decor: How the Late Roman Aristocrat Appeared to His Guests. In E. Gazda (ed.), *Roman Art in the Private Sphere*, 117–134. Ann Arbor: University of Michigan Press.

Frere, Sheppard S. 1982. The Bignor Villa. *Britannia* 13:135–195.

Goodburn, Roger 1979. *Chedworth: The Roman Villa*. London.

Haverfield, R. 1914. Roman Silver in Northumberland. *Journal of the Roman Society* 4:1–12.

Henig, Martin 1986a. Ita intellexit numine inductus tuo: some personal interpretations of deity in Roman religion. In Martin Henig and A. King (eds), *Pagan Gods and Shrines of the Roman Empire*, 159–169. Oxford University Committee for Archaeology Monograph 8.

Henig, Martin 1986b. Late Roman Mosaics in Britain: Myth and Meaning. *Mosaic* 13:13–20.

Hinks, R. 1933. *Catalogue of Greek, Etruscan and Roman Paintings in the British Museum*. London.

Hoare, R. C. 1819. *History of Ancient Wiltshire, Part 2*, Roman Aera. London.

Hodder, Ian R. 1986. *Reading the Past*. Cambridge: Cambridge University Press.

Ingram, J. 1849. Notices of the Mosaic Pavement discovered at Thruxton, Hants. in 1823. *Proceedings of the Royal Archaeological Institute*, Vol. of the Wilts. and Salisbury meeting, 241–245.

Jesnick, I. 1989. Animals in the Orpheus Mosaics. *Mosaic* 16:9–13.

Ling, R. 1982. Mosaics and Murals. *Mosaic* 7:26–28.

Lysons, S. 1817. *Roman Antiquities at Woodchester*.

McWhirr, Alan 1986. *Houses in Roman Cirencester*. Cirencester Excavations 3.

Merrifield, R. 1986. The London Hunter-God. In Martin Henig and Anthony King (eds.) *Pagan Gods and Shrines of the Roman Empire*. Oxford University Committee for Archaeology Monograph 8, 85–92.

Miller, Daniel 1982. Structures and Strategies: an Aspect of the Relationship between Social Hierarchy and Cultural Change. In Ian Hodder (ed.) *Symbolic and Structural Archaeology*, 89–98. Cambridge: Cambridge University Press.

Millett, Martin 1990. *The Romanization of Britain*. Cambridge: Cambridge University Press.

Morphy, Howard (ed.) 1989. *Animals into Art*. London: Unwin Hyman.

Neal, D. S. 1981. *Roman Mosaics in Britain*. Gloucester.

Nichols, W. L. 1938. *The Roman Villa at Newton St. Loe*.

Painter, K. S. 1977. *The Mildenhall Treasure: Roman Silver from East Anglia*. London: British Museum Publications.

Preston Blier, S. 1987. *The Anatomy of Architecture.* Cambridge: Cambridge University Press.

Rawes, B. 1977. A Romano-British Site on the Portway. *Glevensis* 11.

Reece, Richard 1980. Town and Country: the End of Roman Britain. *World Archaeology* 12 (1):77–92.

Rivet, A. L. F. (ed.) 1969. *The Roman Villa in Britain.* London: Routledge.

Salway, Peter 1984. *Roman Britain.* Oxford: Oxford University Press.

Scott, Eleanor 1990. Romano-British Villas and the Social Construction of Space. In Ross Samson (ed.), *The Social Archaeology of Houses,* 149–172. Edinburgh: Edinburgh University Press.

Scott, Sarah 1989. Symbols of Power and Nature: a Contextual Approach to the Orpheus Mosaics of Fourth Century Roman Britain. Unpublished BSc. dissertation, University of Leicester.

Scott, Sarah 1991. An Outline of a New Approach for the Interpretation of Romano-British Villa Mosaics, and Some Comments on the Possible Significance of the Orpheus Mosaics of Fourth Century Roman Britain. *Journal of Theoretical Archaeology* 2:29–35.

Shanks, Michael and Christopher Tilley 1987. *Social Theory and Archaeology.* Cambridge: Polity Press.

Smith, D. J. 1969. The Mosaic Pavements. In A. L. F. Rivet (ed.), *The Roman Villa in Britain,* 71–125. London: Routledge.

Stead, Ian M. 1976. *Excavations at Winterton Roman Villa and other Roman Sites in N. Lincolnshire.* Department of the Environment (Report No. 9).

Stevens, C. E. 1933. *Sidonius Apolinaris and His Age.* Oxford.

Thebert, Y. 1987. Private Life and domestic Architecture in Roman Africa. In P. Veyne (ed.), *A History of Private Life,* 1, *From Pagan Rome to Byzantium,* 319–409.

Todd, Malcolm 1978. Villas and Romano-British Society. In M. Todd (ed.), *Studies in the Romano-British Villa,* 197–208. Leicester: Leicester University Press.

Toynbee, Jocelyn M. C. 1962. *Art In Roman Britain.*

Toynbee, Jocelyn M. C. 1964. *Art in Britain under the Romans.*

Walters, B. 1981. Littlecote. *Current Archaeology* 80:264–268.

Walters, B. 1982. Fourth-Century 'Orphic' Halls in Britain. *Mosaic* 7:23–26.

Wedlake, W. J. 1982. *The Excavation of the Shrine of Apollo at Nettleton, Wiltshire, 1956–1971.* London: Society of Antiquaries.

Wheeler, R. E. Mortimer and Tessa V. Wheeler 1932. *Report on the Excavations of the Prehistoric, Roman and Post Roman Site in Lydney Park, Gloucestershire.* Oxford: Society of Antiquaries of London.

9

ROMANS AND BRITONS ON THE NORTHERN FRONTIER: A THEORETICAL EVALUATION OF THE ARCHAEOLOGY OF RESISTANCE

Bernice Kurchin

Despite the multiplicity of approaches in the revolt against strict positivism in archaeological theory, all of them share a focus on human agency as a necessary part of explanation. Nowhere is this more apparent than in the recent literature concerning complex societies, relations of inequality and particularly studies of power and dominance where, according to Daniel Miller, 'agency and resistance are integral to their definition' (1989: 64).

Archaeology has long been concerned with the cultural remains of dominant ideologies, but has understood them normatively rather than in terms of conflict. When we consider relations of domination and resistance, the focus turns from normative systems of interaction to the behaviour of individuals.

The subject is most often subsumed under the broader categories of gender and colonialism, and often the first is seen as a subtopic of the second under the Marxist paradigm of imperialism and female subordination being peculiar to capitalism or class societies. Gender studies are an outgrowth of the feminist movement, with its concomitant need to develop a 'herstory' for women, similar to that of minority peoples who were without history and known to the present only through the voice of colonial usurpers. The intense focus on colonialism however seems to be the result of theoretical realignment in a period when both imperialism and the appearance of being aligned with imperial policy are politically incorrect. Thus, archaeological interest in colonialism is shifting away from questions of extraction, taxation, and urbanisation, where culture change is presented as something imposed from above by the intrusive power. Instead a discourse between domination and resistance is being analysed as a source of cultural transformation.

Both these terms – domination and resistance – need some clarification. To paraphrase Randall McGuire and Robert Paynter (1991: 8), domination occurs when A tells B what to do and B does it, whether it is in his best interests or not. B's response may be a reaction to force or the threat of force. It is more likely a dialogue in which both A and B acknowledge A's right to dominate in terms of a shared legitimising ideology (Miller 1989; McGuire and Paynter 1991).

In the Roman case both factors worked to establish dominance. As Edward Luttwak (1976: 195–200) pointed out, the direct force of the Roman army, and even more, the power of its reputation, served to ensure imperial control. At the same time, the Romans linked the interests of the native elite to their own administration, and acculturation took place through the intercession of the elite with their people (cf. Millett 1990: 82–85).

Resistance is more difficult to define. On the one hand, there is overt resistance. In, for instance, the uprising of AD 118–119 on the northern British frontier or during the Boudiccan revolt, B was acting to remove A's domination. A number of such acts of rebellion have been documented for us by the Romans (Dyson 1971).

A less dramatic form of this can be seen in the creation of what Owen Lattimore called 'interior frontiers' in certain parts of the empire (cf. Dyson 1975: 148), such as inaccessible mountain retreats for bandits, rebels and malcontents (Dyson 1975: 173). It must be noted here, however, that the difference between, for instance, banditry and revolt is not necessarily in the attitude of the provincials, about which we know nothing. It is in the response of the Romans, who chose to record the presence of Dardanian bandits in Moesia but apparently ignored them because they did not interfere with trade, nor were they a threat to the empire (Mócsy 1974: 152). This kind of resistance can be interpreted as useful to the Romans, in fact, because it served to strengthen the propaganda value of the Pax Romana and, through backlash, could reinforce their dominant position.

Most of the recent archaeological literature, however, is concerned with a more covert form of resistance, which might best be characterised as B doing what A says to do, but thumbing his nose at him behind his back. This conflict is enacted in the ideological arena and may never go further than symbolic counter-cultural expressions. Elizabeth Brumfiel has shown how women resisted the negative and subordinating image of themselves propagated by the official Aztec religion by intensifying production of ceramic figurines showing them in the traditional pre-Aztec manner (1989).

Overt resistance may sometimes be difficult to operationalise on the ground. For example, did the Romans destroy Newstead, the Roman fort near Melrose, Scotland, where excavation has revealed deliberate slighting of the walls (Curle 1911) or did the natives attack it? Did this happen during the 'Brigantian revolt' or as part of the abandonment of the Antonine frontier (Richmond 1924)? Nevertheless, the study of overt rebellion is conceptually less problematical than the covert resistance with which most of the current archaeological literature is concerned. The latter is not only hard to operationalise, but there are also difficulties with the way the concept has been applied.

Colonial situations are no less fluid than time. In the nearly four centuries of its existence Britannia changed both politically and economically, as did the empire of which it was a part. The same factions whose interests were served by resistance in the first century may have been just the ones to benefit by the economic changes of the post-Severan period. Martin Millett has shown how the shifting locus of power is reflected in the emergence of new centres of exchange, suggesting as well that new people were benefiting from these changes (1990: 127–37). The tribal elites most likely to support Romanisation in the early years of the province may have been most threatened by the disruptions of the third century.

Although change is less evident in the military zone than in the south, intermarriage between military personnel and northern women was creating a new population of Romano-British, while opportunities to serve in the army at home were increasing for the Britons, making the military presence less provocatively foreign – though not totally – as the centuries passed. Rather than an object of hostile resistance, the army would have become part of the social fabric of the northern community. While the possibility of resistance would not necessarily diminish under new circumstances, both the source and object would be different, a factor which must be considered in any evaluation of colonial interactions.

Having reasons for resistance is not the same thing as having evidence of resistance. McGuire and Paynter (1991: 19) point out that using prehistoric assemblages unsupported by documentation runs the danger of presenting a circular argument where resistance is assumed and material culture is then used to verify its existence. This is so for the severely limited documentation of the Roman period as well.

There are several reasons to suppose resistance occurred in Britain on both sides of the frontier zone. Historically, the mere presence of a standing army is provocative, and not everyone would have experienced the army as an economic stimulus (cf. Whittaker 1989: 66–69).

Mark Gregson (1982: 21–23) suggested that indigenous land tenure was rooted in social relationships that conflicted with Roman practices. It is quite reasonable to suggest that northern British land tenure differed from Roman, and that changes in these relationships would not be well received by all parts of native society. If nothing else, a mixed subsistence economy with considerable open pasture might conflict with the carefully surveyed land boundaries of the Roman administration. Presumably, Roman pacification also put an end to cattle raiding, which could have been central to the native prestige economy (Kurchin 1983).

If we believe resistance to have been the case and have reason to expect it, we may tend to see it in all the material we find. Usually, the kind of evidence put forward is negative, that is, lack of acculturation or retention of native cultural traditions is seen as resistance. Andras Mócsy's (1974: 148–49) analysis of the distribution of tombstones and his interpretation of the resurgence of cart burials in 2nd century Pannonia is just such a case. Burial practices are particularly sensitive to ideological transformations, and both resistance and acculturation have been argued from them in New World historical archaeology (Robinson et al. 1985; Axtell 1981). Such data need more critical attention before qualifying as examples of resistance. Since burial data for the Iron Age are nearly non-existent in most parts of Britain (Whimster 1981: 196), and what there is for the Roman period is as likely to be Roman and military as civilian and British, it is currently impossible to assess whether traditional practices were retained or Roman practices adopted by indigenous people, though a closer investigation of the Romano-British burial practices in north-east Yorkshire could be fruitful. Even here, difficulties arise from the context of behaviour which are further explored below.

The continued construction of and residence in Iron Age round houses during the Romano-British period is a phenomenon that can be interpreted as resistance through retention, particularly as villas and town houses are universally accepted as examples of *romanitas*. If the rural Britons did consciously resist such acculturation, it may have been in the deliberate retention of traditional house forms, but how do we distinguish resistance to Roman architectural styles from cultural conservatism, or from the poverty that seems so prevalent in the north?

The Romans did not enforce acculturation, nor did they require anyone to act like a Roman, particularly since most of the material aspects of being Romanised were expensive. In Britain, Romanisation was a prestige good fitting nicely into an established pattern of social interactions and leaving those without prestige living on their traditional Iron Age farms in round houses. That the northern environment was not particularly conducive to the production of significant agricultural surpluses is suggested by the relative paucity of late pre-Roman Iron Age material data.

In addition, Millett has noted (1990: 100–101), and I have argued elsewhere (1989: 11–12), that the administrative role which enhanced the status and wealth of the southern and eastern elites was absorbed by the military in the north, resulting in a far less Romanised civilian landscape.

Acculturation itself is a fairly flexible term. Roman syncretism and eclecticism (Henig 1984: 210–14) left room for broad interpretations of what being a good Roman meant. Nowhere is this more apparent than in the Romanised Celtic gods, the Celticised Roman gods or Romano-Celtic Mithraism. One could argue that the elongated Celtic faces of many of the gods (Henig 1984) and the Celtic clothing worn by the goddesses (Allason-Jones 1989) are a form of resistance to religious conversion but they could be just as well understood as the Roman dieties being made local or those of the barbarians being 'civilised'.

Both acculturation and resistance are actions situated in particular contexts. Even for the elites, acting in the new style in public would not negate using traditional forms in private. Lindsay Allason-Jones has suggested that women may have fared better in native society than under colonial jurisdiction, particularly those who found themselves living in towns (1989a: 191). Since women were not part of the public arena as defined by Romans, their retention of native clothing styles, jewelry, textiles, even cooking technology could only be considered as private action. Does conservatism in the domestic arena constitute resistance or a separation of contexts: public being Roman, and domestic being native?

An interesting phenomenon that could be understood here as resistance in the public arena is the unusual distribution of earrings throughout the empire, noted by Allason-Jones (1989b). Traditionally worn by both men and women of the eastern provinces, they were assumed to be worn only by women in Britannia. But Allason-Jones discusses in this volume the lack of evidence for such an assumption. In fact if they were worn by both men and women, the fashion is counter to classical taste – Allason-Jones suggests it might not have been quite respectable (1989b: 36) – and may indicate an interesting cultural alignment with the exotic, the non-Roman, on the part of some Britons. Alternatively, it may indicate a much more inclusive definition of what is Roman on the part of the provincial Britons – a different concept from that of the Roman elite.

This last example illustrates what is here considered the overriding difficulty with defining resistance in the archaeological record. Understanding resistance means reading not only the symbolic content of an artifact but the intent behind its use. While I accept the claim of Mary Beaudry et al. (1991: 174) that almost all material objects have symbolic and social meanings which mediate their use – as, for instance samian ware might be understood in the context of upward mobility – the same objects can mean different things to different people, and their meaning is rarely our meaning. The really convincing studies of artifacts as objects of resistance are done in settings where written sources confirm or support symbolic interpretation. Where there is a shared or homogeneous system of meaning in the culture we are studying, we could probably come to a consensus of interpretation. In a complex situation such as the northern frontier, with Romans, Britons, and soldiers of various ethnicities, and little likelihood of perfect communication between them, how are we supposed to understand and choose from among the array of possible meanings?

Finally, not even texts can completely elucidate the intent of the actors in these cases. Documentation is data filtered through elite perspectives (McGuire and Paynter 1991; Kurchin 1989). Since covert resistance enables a far wider range of expression than overt confrontation, it is possible that it is not recognised by the dominant authority for what it is. Or, perhaps more likely, it is recognised but ignored as irrelevant or even as behaviour useful to the power structure (Miller 1989: 68). Finally, resistance may reside in alternative perspectives or thoughts even as the behaviour gives the appearance of conformity, leaving no evidence for resistance in the archaeological record. Thus, we need to question whether resistance can be so distinguished if B alone understands his actions as such.

This paper is not meant to argue the glories of *romanitas* or decry the docility of the northern Britons. Rather it is a lament for the limits of archaeology. Material data do not readily yield answers to questions of intent. The great advantage of our discipline – time depth, or deja vu as Miller (1989: 78) calls it – may be able in the long term to identify those elements of a culture resistant to change or acculturation in a colonial situation. Interpretation of human agency, in the short term at least, suffers from indeterminacy. The linkage with the archaeological record weakens as we move from questions of action, to meaning, to motivation, to intent, though all are aspects of agency. Without supporting documents, which are flawed by their own biases, or several data sets pointing to the same conclusion, it may be nearly impossible to present a testable archaeological argument for any but the most overt resistance.

ACKNOWLEDGEMENTS ————————

This paper is a by-product of research sponsored by the Wenner-Gren Foundation For Anthropological Research. I am grateful to Professors Gregory A. Johnson and Thomas H. McGovern of Hunter College, CUNY for reading and commenting on drafts of this work and most grateful to David Yoon of The Graduate Center, CUNY for his critical comments and editorial assistance at every stage. The mistakes are my own.

References

Allason-Jones, Lindsay 1989a. *Women in Roman Britain*. London: British Museum.

Allason-Jones, Lindsay 1989b. *Earrings in Roman Britain*. Oxford: British Archaeological Reports (British Series 201).

Axtell, James 1981. The Acculturation of Native Funerals in Colonial North America. *The European and the Indian*, 110–128. New York: Oxford Univeristy Press.

Beaudry, Mary, Lauren J. Cook and Stephen A. Mrozowski 1991. Artifacts and Active Voices: Material Culture as Social Discourse. In Randall H. McGuire and Robert Paynter (eds), *The Archaeology of Inequality*, 150–191. Oxford: Blackwell.

Brumfiel, Elizabeth 1990. Figurines and the Aztec State: the Case for and against Ideological Domination. Paper presented at the 89th annual meeting of the American Anthropological Association. New Orleans.

Curle, James A. 1911. *A Roman Frontier Post and its People: The Fort at Newstead, near Melrose*. London.

Dyson, Stephen L. 1971. Native Revolts in the Roman Empire. *Historia* 20:239–274.

Dyson, Stephen L. 1975. Native Revolt Patterns in the Roman Empire. In H. Temporini and W. Haase (eds), *Aufsteig und Niedergang der römischen Welt* II:3, 138–175.

Frere, Sheppard S. 1987. *Britannia: a History of Roman Britain*. London: Routledge and Kegan Paul.

Gregson, Mark 1988. The Villa as Private Property. In Keith Branigan and David Miles (eds), *The Economies of Romano-British Villas*, 21–33. Sheffield: J. R. Collis Publications.

Henig, Martin 1984. *Religion in Roman Britain*. London: Batsford.

Kurchin, Bernice 1983. The Effect of Colonization on the Votadini: a Settlement Pattern Analysis. MA Thesis, Department of Anthropology. Hunter College, C.U.N.Y.

Kurchin, Bernice 1989. Native Speeches in the Latin Tongue: the Archaeological Evidence for Imperial Abuse in Roman Britain. Paper presented at the annual meeting of the American Anthropological Association. Washington, D.C.

Luttwak, Edward 1976. *The Grand Strategy of the Roman Empire*. Baltimore: Johns Hopkins University Press.

McGuire, Randall H. and Robert Paynter 1991. The Archaeology of Inequality: Material Culture, Domination and Resistance. In Randall H. McGuire and Robert Paynter (eds), *The Archaeology of Inequality*, 1–27. Oxford: Blackwell.

Miller, Daniel 1989. The Limits of Dominance. In Daniel Miller, Michael Rowlands, Christopher Tilley (eds), *Domination and Resistance*, 63–79. London: Unwin Hyman.

Millett, Martin 1990. *The Romanization of Britain*. Cambridge: Cambridge University Press.

Mócsy, Andras 1974. *Pannonia and Upper Moesia: A History of the Middle Danube Provinces of the Roman Empire*. London: Routledge and Kegan Paul.

Richmond, Ian A. 1924. The Relation of the Fort at Newstead to Scottish History, AD 80–180. *Proceedings of the Society of Antiquaries of Scotland* 58:309–321.

Richmond, Ian A. 1958. Ancient Geographical Sources for Britain North of the Cheviots. In Ian A. Richmond (ed.), *Roman And Native in North Britain*, 131–149. Edinburgh: Nelson.

Robinson, Paul A, Marc A. Kelley and Patricia Rubertone 1985. Interpretations from a Seventeenth Century Narraganset Cemetery. In William W. Fitzhugh (ed.), *Cultures in Contact*, 107–130. Washington, D.C.: Smithsonian Institution.

Steer, Kenneth A. 1958. Roman and Native in North Britain: the Severan Reorganization. In Ian A. Richmond (ed.), *Roman and Native in North Britain*, 91–111. Edinburgh: Nelson.

Whimster, Rowan 1981. *Burial Practices in Iron Age Britain*. Oxford: British Archaeological Reports (British Series 90 i and ii).

Whittaker, C. R. 1983. Trade and the Frontiers of the Roman Empire. In Peter Garnsey and C. R. Whittaker (eds), *Trade and Famine in Classical Antiquity*, 110–127. Cambridge: Cambridge Philological Society (Supplement 8).

10

Shoppers' Paradise: Consumers in Roman Britain

Iain Ferris

'I often wonder that it should be so dull', Catherine Morland said of history in 'Northanger Abbey', 'for a great deal of it must be invention'. Conversely, can the invented world, the realm of the novelist, contain historical insights, explanations and models that could be of use to the archaeologist or historian in writing his or her own academic narratives? Christopher Evans, in his paper 'Digging with the Pen: Novel Archaeologies and Literary Traditions', wrote that 'while inspiring, literature and literary criticism hold no ready-made formulae for the social sciences' (Evans 1989: 204) but also noted the existence of a fictional genre, which he called 'post-holocaust' or 'terrestrial' science fiction, in which reflections 'upon the role of material culture and identity' were prevalent (Evans 1989: 201). He interpreted such examples as instances of the individual bodying forth order out of chaos, 'the very solidity of things . . . appeal[ing] beyond the purely sentimental inasmuch as they embody time and can be personally/culturally symbolic' (Evans 1989: 201). The matter of the novel itself having the potential to be an archaeology of contemporary material culture was not considered.

In this paper it is proposed, firstly, to examine a number of novels that each evoke and enshrine the essence of the material culture of their particular era and which, in so doing, create visions of those eras which could be said to constitute historical documents. In these novels the authors consider the role of objects in relation to the people who bought, used and discarded them and thus indirectly allude to the broader society or culture in which these various transactions take place. Secondly, attention will be focused on a number of anthropological and sociological studies of consumer societies, highlighting the mechanics and processes of consumption, before finally turning to examine the potential relevance of the novelistic and/or anthropological approach to the theoretical treatment of consumption in the Romano-British period.

The solid and ubiquitous material culture of Victorian Britain, a society so perfectly described by Henry James as 'the Empire of Things', can be evoked no better than through the writings of Dickens, Thackeray or James himself. In 'The Spoils of Poynton' James recounts the battle between Mrs Gereth, a widow, and her son over the contents of Poynton Park. To Mrs Gereth 'things were . . . the sum of the world' (James 1897: 20) and 'the old golds and brasses, old ivories and bronzes, the fresh old tapestries and deep old damasks threw out a radiance in which [she] saw in solution all her old loves and patiences, all her old tricks and triumphs' (James 1897: 43). The contents of the house were not merely an assemblage of artefacts but were rather 'the record of a life . . . written in great syllables of colour and form, the tongues of other countries and the hands of rare artists' (James 1897: 18–19); their very essence could not be captured or tamed in an inventory for it was rather embodied in 'a presence, a perfume, a touch' (James 1897: 180).

A different approach to the material world can be seen in Georges Perec's novel *Les Choses*, translated as *Things. A Story of the Sixties*, in which the novel's protagonists are realised, and their characters defined, almost entirely through an examination of their relationship with material culture. Their elevation from a bohemian student existence to the world of work was marked by an accompanying change in material lifestyle; 'they . . . burned what they had previously worshipped: the witches' mirrors, the chopping-blocks, those stupid little mobiles, the radiometers, the multi-coloured pebbles, the hessian panels adorned with expressive squiggles' (Perec 1965: 33–34) and they moved on to objects 'which only the taste of the day decreed to be beautiful: imitation Epinal pseudo-naive cartoons, English-style etchings, agates, spun-glass tumblers, neo-primitive paste jewellery, para-scientific apparatus' (Perec 1965: 33). Later in the novel, out of work, they leave France and take up teaching posts in Tunisia. While still surrounded by their possessions, the material paraphernalia that had previously given their lives meaning now seemed curiously alienating in a new environment and though it still 'exuded a little warmth' it was more of a

barrier than a bridge. Their host culture did not entice them and they
bought nothing 'because they did not feel drawn to these things'. In
essence 'it was wanting that had been all their existence' (Perec 1965: 119).

A more recent novel, Nicholson Baker's 'The Mezzanine', approaches the
America of rampant consumerism and packaging-overload with a micro-
scopic eye, much of the book consisting of a stream-of-consciousness, ob-
sessive, inner dialogue about the design and significance of, for instance,
drinking straws, shoelaces, sugar-sachets, milk cartons and so on. Billed as
the story of one man's lunch-hour, the apparent triviality of these musings
conceals a razor-sharp and amusing critique of the cult of the disposable
and the hidden meanings of sometimes banal objects. To the narrator
'what was central and what was incidental end up exactly reversed' (Baker
1988: 92). Baker's investigation of the object as cultural sign or signifier is
not a new phenomenon and perhaps the best examples of an almost ob-
sessive search into the ramifications of the object as symbol are to be found
in the works of Kafka, though these will not be considered here.

Some writers use objects to create a stage setting in an unashamedly
nostalgic manner which triggers, when successful, recognition and response in the reader. One recent example will here suffice. In 'Motorama
1954' Bill Morris, while he fails to create a a particularly engrossing or convincing drama, sets the scene with a virtual archaeology of the Fifties consumer paradise of finned-automobiles, ideal kitchens, cocktail and bar paraphernalia and deep-piled carpets, a mixture of the ubiquitous, and at times
absurd, labour-saving devices of the day and the merely fashionable object
or status symbol (Morris 1992).

Perec, Baker and Morris all owe something to the work of anthropolog-
ists, sociologists and consumer researchers whose approaches to material
culture through personal observation and interview provide a dimension
alien to the kind of object-led study to which many archaeologists are, by
necessity, restricted. In particular, Douglas and Isherwood (1978) in *The
World of Goods. Towards an Anthropology of Consumption* and Csikszentmihalyi and Rochberg-Halton (1981) in *The Meaning of Things. Domestic
Symbols and the Self* have shown that an understanding of the motives
behind the acquisition of goods is crucial to an understanding of the wider
social and cultural world, and vice-versa, for the two cannot properly be
separated and it is perhaps unfortunate that we so often study the finds
from, for instance, Roman Britain in splendid isolation. It has been said
that 'consumption is the very arena in which culture is fought over and
licked into shape' (Douglas and Isherwood 1978: 57). 'Goods . . . make and

maintain social relationships' (Douglas and Isherwood 1978: 60), and 'objects . . . serve to express dynamic processes within people, among people, and between people and the total environment. These processes might lead to either a more and more specific differentiation or increasing integration' (Csikszentmihalyi and Rochberg-Halton 1981: 43).

An interdisciplinary approach to the analysis of consumption, interpreting patterns discerned by the study of basic historical data in the form of probate inventories – taken at the time of death and recording the household and/or trade goods of the deceased – has been taken by Lorna Weatherill in her book, *Consumer Behaviour and Material Culture in Britain 1660–1760*, (Weatherill 1988), and I have suggested elsewhere that this study could provide a model for similar work on the material culture of Roman Britain (Ferris forthcoming). While the value of any model lies in the quantity and quality of the available data against which it can be tested, as Millett has pointed out our reticence to undertake theoretical studies of this kind seems untenable given the undoubted value of the database from Roman Britain (Millett 1990a).

Weatherill's analysis of her data allowed her to discuss a number of broader issues; both hierarchical and social ones, such as the roles of status, occupation and wealth in the processes of consumption, as well as geographical ones such as the significance of place of residence, forms of regional variation and the contrast between town and country. These discussions allowed for some analysis and perspective of changes over time, leading to an appreciation of the processes behind the spread of new goods throughout society. Time does not allow here for a full examination of the potential worth of a model based on Weatherill's work transposed back to Roman Britain but one or two parts of that model will be discussed, as they suggest that though obviously objects listed in inventories or objects recovered by archaeological excavation have different values, the broad framework of interpretation can still be applied.

Weatherill found surprisingly that consumption hierarchies and social hierarchies did not completely correspond, as might have been expected, with traders and merchants being higher in the consumption hierarchy, that is tending to be the earliest possessors of new types of goods, than the gentry and others of a higher social status, indicating that the oft-quoted theory of social emulation and display as a dynamic force behind the acquisition and ownership of certain types of new goods is perhaps too simplistic.

Visually, the role of the new object as status symbol cannot be better expressed than in the Bellini painting 'The Feast of the Gods', finished by Titian in 1514, in which the gods dine not off gold and silver plate but off Chinese blue and white porcelain, still a rarity in Europe at that time.

In Roman Britain we can, perhaps, map the possible routes for the introduction of certain types of key Roman goods by reconstructing the information-processing network of the time. Jeremy Evans, in his study of literacy in Roman Britain as reflected in the distribution of graffiti (Evans 1988), found that there were no great regional variations in this distribution but considerable variations depending on the class of sites represented, with a hierarchy of basic literacy declining from forts and towns to villas and other rural sites or settlements. 'There is a very real suggestion that villas may occupy a lower position in the social and economic hierarchy than the towns' (Evans 1988: 202).

Does the poor showing of the villas in this study suggest, as with Weatherill's findings on the secondary position of the gentry in the consumption hierarchies of her period, that there is some doubt as to the role of villa occupiers as influential social innovators in Roman Britain?

The second point be to raised here concerns Weatherill's findings on regional patterns of consumption and the possible explanations for regional differences. While she could not fully develop the theme, due to the limitations imposed by the nature of the evidence, she noted that 'attitudes to consumption and material goods can usefully be examined at a regional level, for in some areas people may have preferred to spend their resources on special occasions rather than in acquiring household durables' (Weatherill 1988: 45), and that in Scotland, for which there exists other documentary sources that can supplement the evidence of the inventories, there are well-documented instances of such conspicuous expenditure. 'Here surplus was consumed in excessive food and drink on a few occasions, rather than on durable goods or even clothing, again characteristic of a 'traditional' attitude to consumption' (Weatherill 1988: 67).

The general question of the regionality of cultures in Roman Britain is a topic that has been relatively understudied. Here I will limit discussion to a brief examination of one example only, that is the situation in the northern military zone. Here there existed not one but four distinct cultures; Roman culture, a distinct and separate Roman military culture, the indigenous local culture, and the culture of the *vicani* who were dependent on the military but who negotiated the space between the two dominant and predominant cultures of Roman and native. It has been suggested that the creation of this situation was brought about by the interplay between two strands of colonial policy at work in the north, one encouraging cultural change but controlling the speed and nature of that change, and the other being the practice of social and cultural isolationism on the part of the immigrants, leading to maintained 'separate development' though under a unitary political and economic control (Higham 1989: 153). Millett though has warned of the dangers of assuming the existence of a comprehensive and unswerving policy of Romanisation; there were, perhaps, more elements of laissez-faire than social-engineering at play (Millett 1990b). In any case, other studies have indicated that the army was not an agent for a policy of Romanisation; rather, this was a separate civil and, presumably, emulative process (Blagg 1980; Evans 1988: 331–33).

The nature of the cultural intercourse between Roman and native in the north has been variously surmised. Bennett saw little or no contact between the two dominant cultures and indeed adopted the idea of a more-or-less seamless indigenous culture with a lifestyle and material culture that changed little from the Iron Age to the post-Roman period. He noted that some absences of Roman goods on native sites 'might indicate a conscious rejection of these goods by the indigenes' (Bennett 1983: 217) or that 'they could not afford such goods' (Bennett 1983: 209). Higham, looking at the area north of the Tees, thought that the local indigenous peoples 'were denied access to provincial civilisation even if some among them perceived a need to adopt it' (Higham 1989: 169) and that in the light of this 'the process of acculturation was thereby severely limited' (Higham 1989: 209). Once more, he considered the possibility of exclusion through poverty and noted that 'the process of pauperisation in many areas, particularly west of the Pennines, is reflected in the failure of the less well-placed communities to attract later prehistoric metalwork' (Higham 1989: 160).

In her study of Roman and native interaction in Northumberland, Lindsay Allason-Jones found that a number of small prestige items of Roman origin, such as intaglios, appeared on native sites but that few metal objects from the same source were present. However, she goes on to note that the later prehistoric culture of the area was also relatively free of such items and that it was 'probable that north of the Tyne wealth was calculated in terms of cattle or by even more intangible means. Perhaps they concentrated on wine, women and song rather than on decorated metalwork' (Allason-Jones 1991: 3), a point also raised by Bennett, who suggested a possible penchant for goods that leave little or no trace in the archaeological record, and by Hingley, who suggested that power, status or prestige among native Romano-Britains could have been manifested by, amongst other things, something as intangible and undetectable as the control of followers (Hingley 1989: 145–47).

Weatherill's identification of regional or local, but otherwise well-integrated, cultures, which through tradition retained patterns of consumption based more upon ostentatious, and often relatively intangible, consumption through display or ceremony rather than on a lower-level acquisition of goods, and Allason-Jones' evidence for perhaps a similar set of cultural priorities in the Roman north are interesting to contrast and connect. However, it is almost impossible to fully define the role played in the mechanics of consumption in Roman Britain by the interplay between the differing value systems of the Roman and Celtic worlds. The lack of any satisfactory method of gauging the level of poverty, and its effects upon the native population in the Roman north, also make the connection difficult to verify on anything other than a theoretical basis. While poverty does undoubtedly lead to cultural exclusion and dispossession at a certain level of society, the poor can also, consciously or unconsciously, use goods as social fences rather than bridges with the construction of a 'culture of poverty', a term first coined by Oscar Lewis in the 1950s (Lewis 1959),in which spending on alcohol, on non-essentials and on conspicuous display, rather than on material goods and often even on essentials, is marked.

In the native cultures of the Roman north we may, in many cases, be looking at sites or settlements so low in the social hierarchy that to use them as indicators of negative contact between Roman and native may be misleading; such sites would be part of what Richard Reece has dubbed 'the sub-culture' of Romanisation, where little or no cultural change over time should indeed be expected (Reece 1990: 32). The true measure of poverty is not in possessions but in the degree of social involvement and Allason-Jones' data, leading her to surmise a considerable traffic of goods from native to Roman, seem to suggest that, leaving aside the very poor, on a regional basis there is an indication of a level of social involvement in the north perhaps over and above that required simply to satisfy the fulfilment of tax obligations. This brings to mind Heisenberg's principle that an observed system inevitably interacts with its observer.

In conclusion, it has been written that for the Roman archaeologist 'fora and baths can tell more of ideology and symbolism than can seeds and sherds' (Jones 1987: 47), but in Roman Britain, by necessity of survival, the ornaments from the period block our view of the architecture. This paper has attempted to suggest that there may be value in the application of anthropologically and sociologically derived models of consumption to the finds data from Roman Britain, and that more imaginative approaches to the writing of archaeological texts might result from a greater awareness of the construction of literary narratives. As Ralph Waldo Emerson wrote, 'the poet, by an ulterior intellectual perception, gives [things] a power which makes their old use forgotten, and puts eyes and a tongue into every dumb and inanimate object'. Judging from the traditional approach to the study of artefacts from Roman Britain taken by the most recent book on the subject, with few attempts to look outside the geographical or chronological limits of the study, one would think that little had changed since the days of Collingwood and Richmond. There is a potential value in a more theoretical approach to the material culture of Roman Britain and in a move on from studies which are largely, to quote Stephen Spender in another context, 'time-obsessed, time-tormented, as though beaten with rods of restless days' (Spender 1951: 137).

ACKNOWLEDGEMENTS ————

I would like to thank Lynne Bevan, Jane Evans and Jeremy Evans for commenting on a draft of this paper.

Bibliography

Allason-Jones, Lindsay 1991. Roman and Native Interaction in Northumberland. In Maxfield and Dobson (eds) 1991, 1–5.

Baker, Nicholson 1988. *The Mezzanine*. Cambridge: Granta Books.

Barrett, John C., Andrew P. Fitzpatrick, and Lesley Macinnes, (eds), 1989. *Barbarians and Romans in North-west Europe from the Later Republic to Late Antiquity*. Oxford: British Archaeological Reports (International Series 471).

Bennett, Julian 1983. The End of Roman Settlement in North England. In Chapman and Mytum (eds) 1983, 205–232.

Blagg, Thomas and Martin Millett (eds). 1990. *The Early Roman Empire in the West*.

Chapman, John C. and Harold C. Mytum (eds) 1983. *Settlement in North Britain, 1000BC-AD1000*. Oxford: British Archaeological Reports (British Series 118).

Csikszentmihalyi, Mihaly and Eugene Rochberg-Halton 1981. *The Meaning of Things. Domestic Symbols and the Self*.

Douglas, Mary and Baron Isherwood 1978. *The World of Goods. Towards an*

Anthropology of Consumption.

Emerson, Ralph Waldo 'The Poet', in *The Best of Ralph Waldo Emerson.* Edited by G. S. Haight 1941. New York.

Evans, Christopher 1989. Digging with the Pen: Novel Archaeologies and Literary Traditions. *Archaeological Review from Cambridge* 8(2):185–211.

Evans, Jeremy 1987. Graffiti and the Evidence of Literacy and Pottery Use in Roman Britain. *Archaeological Journal* 144:191–204.

Ferris, Iain M. forthcoming. The Image is a Drawbridge. Objects as Ideas in Roman Britain. Proceedings of the Conference 'Finds from the Imperial West'.

Higham, Nicholas J. 1989. Roman and Native in England North of the Tees; Acculturation and its Limitations. In Barrett, Fitzpatrick and Macinnes (eds) 1989, 153–174.

Hingley, Richard 1989. *Rural Settlement in Roman Britain.* London: Seaby

James, Henry 1897. *The Spoils of Poynton.* (1963) Harmondsworth: Penguin.

Jones, Richard F. J. 1987. A False Start? The Roman Urbanization of Western Europe. *World Archaeology* 19(1):47–57.

Jope, E. M. 1973. The Transmission of New Ideas: Archaeological Evidence for Impact and Dispersal. *World Archaeology* 4(3):368–373.

Lewis, Oscar 1959. *Five Families Mexican Case Studies in the Culture of Poverty.* New York..

Maxfield, Valerie A. and Michael J. Dobson (eds) 1991. Roman Frontier Studies. *Proceedings of the XVth International Congress of Roman Frontier Studies.*

Millett, Martin 1990a. *The Romanization of Britain: an Essay in Archaeological Interpretation.* Cambridge: Cambridge University Press.

Millett, Martin 1990b. Historical Issues and Archaeological Interpretations. In Blagg and Millett (eds) 1990, 35–41.

Morris, Bill 1992. Motorama 1954. In 'We're So Happy!', Granta 38: 13–86.

Perec, Georges 1965. *Things. A Story of the Sixties.* Translated by D. Bellos (1991). London: Harvill.

Reece, Richard 1990. Romanization: a Point of View. In Blagg and Millett (eds) 1990, 30–34.

Spender, Stephen 1951. *World Within World.* London: Hamish Hamilton.

Weatherill, Lorna 1988. *Consumer Behaviour and Material Culture in Britain 1660–1760.* London: Methuen.

11

ECONOMY AND SPACE IN ROMAN BRITAIN

Pete Rush

INTRODUCTION ————

I do not intend to give an account of the nature of the Romano-British economy but by re-examining the basis of current thinking my aim is to outline a new strategy through which the chronological development and the geographical variation of the economy can be investigated and placed within the context of Romano-British society as a whole. As I hope to show the present consensus has not only, in effect, limited the questions that have been addressed but also has inherent methodological and theoretical problems. In this paper I shall restrict myself largely to issues of exchange and distribution as these are, perhaps, currently most prominent and it is not possible in the space available to discuss all aspects of the Romano-British economy.

THE CURRENT FRAMEWORK

The current approach to explaining economic phenomena is characterised by a number of interconnected facets: an implicit theoretical base derived from the substantivist brand of functionalism; a constraining framework derived from historical sources; a failure to integrate economics fully with the social sphere and an inadequate conception of spatial relationships.

It was Hodder's 1979 paper that first introduced the substantivist's view of economics to Romano-British archaeology. The ideas outlined in this paper have formed the basis of much subsequent discussion on the question of whether exchange was embedded within social relations or took place through disembedded market mechanisms (e.g. Fulford 1981 and 1989; Millett 1990: 123–26 and 157–80). As a result the nature of the economy appears to have often been presented as one of two possibilities, either embedded or disembedded. This dichotomous characterisation of economics has led to a general failure to attempt to explore in more detail the constitution of the Romano-British economy.

Social relations have largely been seen as acting as constraints upon the distribution of particular artefacts within an embedded economy. Generally, the embeddedness of an exchange system has been demonstrated through the apparent coincidence of the spatial limits of both social groups, particularly tribal areas, and artefact distributions. For example Hodder (1979) suggests a social boundary limited the distribution of Savernake ware in particular directions and Evans (1985 and 1991) makes a similar point in relation to pottery produced in East Yorkshire which for much of the Roman period has a distribution restricted to that region. Clearly, the interaction of economic activity and social relations may be far more complex than this and the evidence of the overlapping distributions of pottery of various types and other material does suggest this to be the case in Roman Britain. Furthermore, the limitation of this approach can be seen in the difficulty of distinguishing a socially constrained distribution from a distribution limited by market economic factors, particularly transport costs.

Although substantivist theory maintains the importance of the role of social factors in exchange the conceptualisation of the relationship between the two has the effect of analytically isolating the economic system from the rest of society. Economic organisation is presented as determined by social relationships and organisation and thus the distribution patterns of particular objects such as certain classes of pottery are treated as abstract entities separate from their specific contexts of occurrence and often without regard for their symbolic, social or practical values. This limits explanation to the level of describing an economy as embedded and prevents further analysis of the inter-relationship of social and economic activity. The implicit functionalist theoretical basis of this perspective also presents problems in accounting for economic change. As it was developed within anthropology functionalism was mainly concerned with the synchronic description and analysis of societies and how social institutions and structures functioned within a particular society to maintain it. This makes external factors, in this case the roles of the Roman army and imperial administration, particularly in the form of taxation and monetary supply, preeminent as causal factors of change in Romano-British economic systems (e.g. Fulford 1989; Middleton 1979). The embedded/disembedded dichotomy is then apparent as a contrast between the continuation of Iron Age exchange patterns and a market economy that develops under the guidance of external Romanising influences. This downplays the possibility of economic and social change being the result of internal societal dynamics.

I want to turn now to consider disembedded market economics. An important question here is how appropriate is it to treat market exchange as analytically separate from the social and political sphere? Economic relations always intersect with social organisation and structure within a society and, hence, cannot be adequately addressed from a theoretical stance that isolates them from each other. A fully disembedded economy would require exchange to take place without any regard for the social and political relationships between the participants and the exchange itself would have no symbolic dimension or meaning beyond what could be accounted for in terms of profit or loss. As Davis (1992) argues, even in a contemporary capitalist society economic activity and exchange have symbolic and social aspects and a price fixing market exchange model is simply inadequate in explaining all economic phenomena.

The readiness with which substantivist economics were accepted into Romano-British archaeology is perhaps linked to the current dominance of an explanatory framework, based on information derived from historical sources, which also emphasises the external origins of societal change within Roman Britain. Archaeological data, rather than being examined in terms of its own content, structure and relationships, has, to some extent, been fitted into a prior historical scheme. This is evident not just as a chronological framework but in the use of references to historical events to provide causal factors to explain perceived changes in material culture (Hingley 1989: 1–3). This has again led to a reliance on external influences to explain societal change and perhaps also to an overemphasis on the more obviously 'Romanised' facets of Roman Britain.

Within this approach to Romano-British exchange systems and economics the mapping and analysis of the distribution of particular artefact types, especially pottery, has played a central role. The reason for this is clear as trade and exchange are only archaeologically visible through recovered material that can be shown to have been transported away from its place of production. The methodological and theoretical approach to space and spatial relationships within distributional analyses occupies a critical place.

Often space has been treated as an isotropic plain that forms an unchanging background to particular distribution patterns. This has been the case not only for spatial studies of pottery but also in investigations of the distributions of different kinds of settlements (Fulford and Hodder 1975; Hodder and Hassall 1971). Spatial relations have been presented as the straight line distances between the locations of the things being studied, and in the case of exchange and economic systems these distances have been presumed to be proportional to transport costs. For example King (1981) has calculated that the cost of transporting samian into Britain from eastern Gaul was approximately double that of importing it from central Gaul but only transport costs appear to have been considered. Other costs such as storage, losses in transit and transference between carriers or modes of transport have been disregarded. This must be an over simplification of the real situation and, therefore, there is a need to take the underlying geography into account.

In large part spatial structures, both in terms of the physical location of sites within the landscape and of the spatial aspects of social relations such as tribal areas, have been seen as prior determining factors of the spatial aspects of exchange systems. In particular, social boundaries have been emphasised as playing an important part in the location of production centres (Millett 1990: 168–69) and in shaping the extent of some exchange or trade networks. This view fails to take into account the role of economic activity as partially constitutive of social relations and boundaries.

If I have been accurate in the assessment I have given then it is clear that we must look for new strategies to explain Romano-British socio-economic phenomena. There is clearly a need to break from substantivist theory and to start analysing the archaeological data in more sophisticated ways independently, to a large extent, of the framework of the historical sources.

OUTLINE OF A NEW STRATEGY

In outlining a new approach to the problem it is first necessary to re-examine what is meant by economics and economic activity. Giddens (1984: 34) points out that 'the sphere of the 'economic' is given by the inherently constitutive role of allocative resources in the structuration of societal totalities'. This perspective makes clear that economics can not be analytically isolated from the other facets of a society and be adequately explained. The essential point is that not only is economic activity always constrained and enabled by the social milieu within which it takes place but that such activity is part of the process of the production and reproduction of the rules and resources that make up the social structure of that society. The question of the embeddedness or disembeddedness of the Romano-British economy is, then, not a particularly informative one to attempt to answer. In fact it has tended to partially obscure the inter-relatedness of economic and social institutions.

Economic activity is inherently spatial in nature, not only in the obvious sense in which all activity must take place within space and time, but that location of the activity is important in explaining and understanding it. Any study of Romano-British economics must therefore take into account as fully as possible the settings of economic activity. The physical attributes of economic space need to be approached methodologically through the transformation of distances into such measures as travel time and transport costs.

We also need to re-orientate our theoretical thinking with respect to space and spatial structures. Space should not simply be thought of as forming a neutral background to the social and economic actions of human agents. As Godelier (1986) has shown through the analysis of numerous ethnographic examples it is not the natural environment that has an effect in shaping economic and social activity but rather the perceptions of environment by those involved. However, the space within which economic activity takes place is not merely determined by the nature of the underlying physical environment as it is perceived but can also be considered as a space defined by social and economic relationships. It should be remembered though, that social and economic action are not merely constrained to follow particular paths by the structure of such space but are reflexively constitutive of it.

How, then, should the investigation of the Romano-British economy proceed? Firstly, the archaeological data needs to be assessed on its own merits before recourse is made to explanation derived from historical sources. This is not to deny that such information can be valuable but to ensure that possible explanations outside its scope are also considered. The economy should always be examined with regard to the other facets of Romano-British society such that the relationships between them can be understood.

Although the inherently spatial character of economic activity makes archaeological distribution data highly appropriate material to use in its explanation from the preceding arguments it should be clear that they should not be used as a basis for explanation in isolation from their contexts.

Account must be taken of the specific nature of the locations that make up the distribution and the relationships between them. It is only by concentrating on the inter-relationships of all the different aspects of material culture that it will be possible to unravel the complex interconnections of economics, social relations and space in Roman Britain.

Finally, it should be noted that although I have largely talked of the Romano-British economy in the singular it is likely that it will be found to consist of a multiplicity of different intersecting economic systems that change through time in different ways in different parts of the province. By adopting this new approach it may be possible to go further in mapping and explaining these phenomena.

References

Davis, John 1992. *Exchange*. Buckingham: Open University Press.

Evans, Jeremy 1985. Aspects of Later Roman Pottery Assemblages in Northern England. Unpublished Ph.D. thesis, University of Bradford.

Evans, Jeremy 1991. Pottery in the Later Roman North: A case study in R. F. J. Jones (ed.), *Britain in the Roman Period: Recent Trends*, 49–512. Sheffield: Collis Publications.

Fulford, Michael G. 1981. Roman Pottery: towards the Investigation of Economic and Social Change. In H. Howard and E. Morris (eds), *Production and Distribution: a Ceramic Viewpoint*, 195–208. Oxford.

Fulford, Michael G. 1989. The Economy of Roman Britain. In Malcolm Todd (ed.), *Research on Roman Britain*, 175–202. London: Britannia (Monograph Series 11).

Fulford, Michael G. and Ian Hodder 1975. A Regression Analysis of Some Late Romano-British Pottery: a Case Study. *Oxoniensia* 39:26–33.

Giddens, Anthony 1984. *The Constitution of Society*. Cambridge: Polity Press.

Godelier, Maurice 1986. *The Mental and the Material*. Verso.

Hingley, Richard 1989. *Rural Settlement in Roman Britain*. London: Seaby.

Hodder, Ian R. 1979. Pre-Roman and Romano-British Tribal Economies. In B. C. Burnham and H. B. Johnson (eds), *Invasion and Response: The Case of Roman Britain*, 189–196. Oxford.

Hodder, Ian R. and M. W. C. Hassall 1971. The Non-random Spacing of Romano-British Walled Towns. *Man* 6:391–407.

King, A. C. 1981. The Decline of Samian Manufacture in the North West Provinces: Problems of Chronology and Interpretation. In A. C. King and Martin Henig (eds), *The Roman West in the Third Century*, 55–78. Oxford.

Middleton, P. S. 1979. Army Supply in Roman Gaul: an Hypothesis for Roman Britain. In B. C. Burnham and H. B. Johnson (eds), *Invasion and Response: the case of Roman Britain*, 81–98. Oxford.

Millett, Martin 1990. *The Romanization of Britain: an Essay in Archaeological Interpretation*. Cambridge: Cambridge University Press.

12

ROMAN POTTERY RESEARCH
FOR THE 1990S

Jason Monaghan

Romano-British pottery studies is an area of research which seems to float in isolation. Within the mainstream textbooks on 'Roman Britain', (e.g. Salway 1981) pottery is either introduced in a selective manner or detailed as an afterthought. Romano-British pottery is generally an under-used resource consigned to the hands of 'specialists' and seemingly understood by few other than that select band. A restricted view of the potential of pottery limits both the status of pottery specialists and the expectations of the reports they produce. These may occasionally draw in statistical tools but rarely progress beyond the most simplistic socio-economic assumptions.

A perusal of the bibliography of any major work on Romano-British pottery will discover few theoretical works quoted. The reverse is also true. Dean Arnold's 'Ceramics and Cultural Process' (1985) has a nineteen page bibliography, yet contains not a single reference to Roman Britain: perhaps the world's most highly investigated area of ceramic study. Its potential for providing raw material for the theoretical archaeologist has been under-exploited, especially in transatlantic publications where the opportunities for cross-fertilisation of ideas are rarely taken up (e.g. Miller 1985). Peacock (1982) applied ethnographic principles in a study of Roman pottery production, but a reverse study is yet to be undertaken.

A division clearly exists between theory and practice. The Dark Ages for Romano-British pottery studies ended circa 1970 and a decade or so of important and innovative publications followed (Gillam 1970; Detsicas

1973; Fulford 1975; Young 1977; etc.). The nineteen eighties, with a few notable exceptions, saw increasing stagnation. Perhaps all the easy questions had been answered, perhaps all the plum subjects had been picked, or perhaps we can blame the changed financial atmosphere. Digging archaeologists allowed objectives in pottery publication to become narrow, often requiring pot specialists to produce bland shopping lists, devoid of comment beyond date ranges and supposed trading links. The results are often as stimulating as a telephone directory and do not do justice to the academic input expended on their creation.

The argument offered to support current practice is that once a site is published, theoreticians can come along, soak up the data and produce something intelligible. Unfortunately, much information is lost between excavation and publication, with technical complexities and advances in methodology limiting the value of archive reports as a research tool. As excavating, cleaning, marking, storing, identifying and quantifying pottery is an expensive procedure, it is cost effective for the researcher on the spot to be allowed put in that extra effort to squeeze the data for all the intellectual benefit it can produce.

Much interest at TRAC 91 and TRAC 92 was attracted to the bottom-up approach to the Roman empire. Both classical sources and conventional archaeological texts concentrate on the military and social elite, their villas, forts and temples, with an diminishing level of interest as they descend the social scale.

An emphasis on the sexy evidence makes for a patchy and disrupted picture of Roman Britain, with periods which saw bursts of construction of public buildings, or of military re-deployment gaining most attention. Archaeological black holes develop where there is a lapse of historical interest, with the mid-third century and the so-called end of Roman Britain as two good examples. It is a circular trap which can ensnare pottery studies. Hostage to the historical approach, a town-based and fort-based chronology falls apart in periods where there is urban desertion or where there is little recognisable military activity. Ceramic typologies can reinforce existing assumptions rather than break new ground and therefore contribute to the problem.

THE ROUTE AHEAD? ————

In the foregoing paragraphs, a somewhat gloomy light has been cast on pottery studies, so what is the route ahead? Renewed interest in the subject is

seen in the growing success of the *Journal of Roman Pottery Studies* and its
establishment as an annual publication following the confident Volume 2
(1989). English Heritage commissioned *The Current State of Romano-British
Pottery Studies* (Fulford and Huddlestone 1991) which although much critic-
ised (Greene 1992), contains the crucial shift of emphasis towards synthetic
and interpretive works. This report also spawned a number of ventures
that should aid first the consolidation, then the advancement of the subject.
Revision of the two aged but venerable guides to pottery research (Webster
1964 and Young 1980) is likewise more probable in the new atmosphere.

The clinical isolation of pottery from synthetic texts has been eased in
offerings by Reece (1988) and by Millet (1990). New thinking is turning
against the shopping-list approach to report writing, with the synthetic
overview finding new favour.

At the end of 1991, A English Heritage funded project began in York, in
which pottery from c. 250 sites is being studied with the deliberate aim of
breaking the circular traps outlined above. Single suburban rubbish-pits,
and areas of waste ground are being considered alongside the impressive
city-centre public buildings. The final report (Monaghan in prep.) will
range beyond the production of a list of dated deposits, or even a typology,
to consider the assemblage as a whole, within its ecological and demographic contexts. Circular arguments are being broken by returning to
basic principles and constructing an internal dated sequence: an approach
more often found in prehistoric archaeology. Dust is being blown off techniques such as seriation and reverence for accepted chronologies and the
sanctity of specialist fine wares is being set aside. By these means, it is
hoped to produce a pottery report for the 1990s.

Borders still remain to be crossed and serious theoretical treatment of the
subject is still a rarity (cf. Going 1992). It is the contention of this paper that
ceramic study is a major route by which serious inroads can be made into
the chronologically and demographically biassed models of Roman Britain.
The cliched value of Romano-British pottery is in its ubiquity, its cheapness
and in consequence its abundance, so even non-use becomes an interesting
feature. Because it occurs in bulk, we have the benefits of being able to
apply a range of mathematical techniques with high degrees of confidence
(Orton and Tyers 1992). It provides a rich database not only for those
studying the Roman period, but for theoreticians interested in wider aspects of ceramic use and material culture. The subject itself is also ideal for
the theoretician to bite into, as there are a wide range of assumptions about
Roman pottery production and use which would benefit from critical study.

ROMAN POTTERY AS A SOCIO-ECONOMIC INDICATOR ──────

Ingenious analysis has managed to show economic competition between pottery industries (Fulford and Hodder 1974), and the literature abounds with free-market assumptions about Roman pottery trade. These assumptions are applicable in some cases, but the overall picture was complicated by various distortions and restraints. Jeremy Evans (1989) has pointed out a tripartite division of Yorkshire pottery distributions, which appear to adhere to tribal boundaries. Paul Buckland, in a lecture delivered to the SGRP in 1990, suggested similar restrictions on the activities of South Yorkshire potters. It is well known that the military took a heavy hand in pottery production and supply (Swan 1994), whether via official contracts or unofficial connivance. The distribution of BB1, BB2 (Gillam 1981) and later, Crambeck ware (Evans 1989) all illustrate this point. This does not look like a free market.

There is also an assumption that pottery is the mark of prosperity and by inference, that pottery production was a path to riches. That this was not always the case can be deduced by considering the BB1 industry of Dorset, Upchurch ware (Monaghan 1987), the BB2 industries of the Thames estuary (ibid.) and East Yorkshire grey wares. The common denominator is swamp or heath close to swamp; the land was fit for little else other than pottery production. One (conventional) conclusion is that entrepreneurs have taken advantage of peace, prosperity and the Roman Way to exploit the pottery market, in particular the military market. Naturally, they sited the potteries on their poorest land. If this had been a recognised way of maximising profit, one would expect to find references to pottery production in the ancient treates aimed at the property-owning class. We do not (Evans 1981: 521), which throws the conclusion into doubt.

Some eighty per cent of ethnographic studies reveal that potters are low-status people who would rather be farmers (Arnold 1985: 193). They are only potters because they have been economically marginalised; this comparison may be totally spurious, but indicates that alternative models exist for Roman Britain. Military and town-based potteries in the post-invasion period gradually gave way to more dispersed rural industries. Couple population pressure with the introduction of villa-estates, land ownership and taxation under Rome and conditions arise in which people might be forced onto marginal land. Pottery production may have been a means of fending off destitution rather than making a quick denarius. This assertion is supported by the dearth of references to potters and pottery in classical literature: where mentioned, both are mean and contemptible. When we identify surges in pottery production we may therefore not looking be looking at peaks of prosperity, but at peaks of social stress.

The conspicuous extravagance evident in the most prominent Roman sites and the profusion of Roman material culture creates the impression of a thriving and sophisticated economy, onto which it is tempting to overlay economic models appropriate to modern, western capitalist nations. The Roman empire was, however, a pre-industrial society, with an economy more analogous to a part-developed third world nation stagnating under an oppressive dictatorship. Pottery 'industries' therefore have to be seen in the correct light, as must economic principles such as supply, demand, price, utility and conceptions of what is a quality and what is an inferior good.

There is an implicit assumption in some studies that the pottery market was consumer-led and there are frequent uses of words such as 'popular' applied to various wares. Producers and consumers of traded fine wares could be separated by great distance and several middlemen, whilst pottery could have spent a number of years in transit and storage before being sold. Although there is evidence for some selectivity at the point of sale (e.g. Hartley and Dickinson in Monaghan 1993) the potential for consumer feedback was limited. The tastes of the inhabitants of northern Britain could have had little bearing on the practices of Central Gaulish Samian potters. Perhaps the only industries truly responding to demand are the very local coarseware industries. In York, a higher proportion of utility vessels, such as lids, was made in grey wares than is found in traded wares. Traded wares such as BB2 comprise a higher ratio of easily transported forms at the point of consumption than point of production (see Table 12.1). Local potters therefore make up the deficit, clearly responding to a gap in the market. There are also instances of 'the public wants what the public gets'. The occurrence of 'African' style pottery production in third-century York can be explained as an act of military policy, but these pots also seem to be used by civilians (Perrin 1981: 90, figs 445–59). A sudden civilian demand for African style casseroles is unlikely, so it may be the case of choice being constrained by availability and availability was determined by the producer. A similar argument may be used to explain the initial enthusiasm for black-burnished ware (Monaghan 1987: 225) or the final adoption of the crude and ugly Calcite-Gritted ware throughout the frontier zone in the 4th century.

This paper does not intend to review the entire Roman economy, but

Table 12.1. Pottery forms as percentage of fabric groups.

	dish	jar	flag.	lid	other	source
York, local greyware	19	61	5	14	1	a
York, BBW	82	18	0	0	0	a
Cooling kiln BB2	50	39	8	0	1	b
Higham kiln BB2	62	38	0	0	0	c

'Jar' includes necked jar/bowls; 'dish' includes deep dish/bowls; 'flag.' = flagons, flasks, etc.
Source: a = Monaghan 1993; b = Monaghan 1987; c = Pollard 1983.

previous assessments (Jones 1974) have indicated that a state of permanent shortages, or at least erratic supply, of commodities was the norm. Following the trauma of invasion and conquest, there would be no real growth in the economy. Demand for pottery could have been totally flat once basic needs were satisfied, leaving little room for entrepreneurs, except at the margins. For the majority of households with static (low) incomes, the demand curve would fluctuate largely in response to changes within that household and its immediate environment. Going (1992: 94–97) recognises little scope for demand fluctuations, with perceived peaks of pottery output being more directly related to the circumstances of production, rather than consumption.

Pottery, especially fine pottery, is often quoted as being a luxury item, with trade as a lucrative result. The intimation is that luxury equals expense, but it is well recognised that Roman pottery was very cheap, with even samian reaching otherwise impoverished sites (Griffiths 1989). It is unlikely that inhabitants of aceramic sites were too poor to afford pottery, it is more probable they did not recognise a need. The question can then be asked, did the wealthy consume more pottery because they could afford to buy more, or simply because the complexities of their lifestyle demanded it? The word 'need' would mean different things to different social groups and it is likely that social attitudes as much as wealth ultimately determined the extent of pottery use. That pottery was not simply a luxury is demonstrated by the gross functionality of much Romano-British coarseware. In contrast, that it was not strictly a necessity is shown by the sudden demise of the craft in the early fifth century. A five-point gradation of pottery demand by households is proposed below. This does not progress strictly by income group, rather it is a progression of social attitudes (Fig. 12.1).

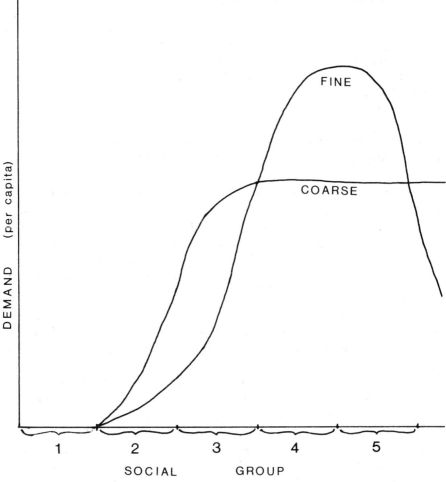

1. Aceramic; has no need for pottery.
2. Acquires basic utility vessels when required, plus the occasional 'poor mans luxury'.
3. Acquires additional vessels, giving a luxury of choice which leads to the possibility of specialised use and a redundancy of forms.
4. Indulges in conspicuous consumption and more rapid replacement of vessels, which will include purchase of novelty items.
5. Regards pottery as an inferior good and replaces it where possible with other materials.

Figure 12.1. Idealised graph plotting household demand (per capita) for pottery against social sophistication. Note that fine and coarse wares are depicted on different scales.

The demand curve for coarse wares would flatten out after point (3) above as their utility declines sharply once basic needs for cooking and storage are filled. Demand for 'fine' wares would increase through point (4), then decline beyond the point they were regarded as vulgar.

CONCLUSION ————

Romano-British pottery encompasses vessels which can be regarded as luxury items and those which are purely functional, but the utility of both was linked to its cheapness. Given adequate access to the markets, pots would be bought when available, with consumer choice being highly limited and exercised at a very local level. There was therefore adequate scope for potteries to be established in response to external socio-economic pressures rather than a sudden 'demand' or an entrepreneurial gamble. Likewise a scenario can be envisaged, whereby industries such as BB2 can lapse without another local rival taking its place.

Having partly decoupled pottery from assumptions of wealth, both in consumption and production, it becomes more of a tool for the study of sociology, demography and ecology, particularly in relation to the humbler parts of the social order. It holds potential for intra-site and inter-site comparisons. This idea is far from new, and can be overplayed, but is often set aside in otherwise commendable site reports. This has been a short excursion into the possibilities of pottery studies. We are in a new decade and we should define new targets and ask new questions of our pottery.

Bibliography

Anderson Anne C. and A. Scott Anderson 1981. *Roman Pottery Research in Britain and North-West Europe.* Oxford: British Archaeological Reports (British Series 123).

Arnold, Dean E. 1985. *Ceramic Theory and Cultural Process.* Cambridge.

Detsicas, Alec P. (ed.) 1973. *Current Research in Romano-British Coarse Pottery.* London: Council for British Archaeology (Research Report 10).

Evans, A. K. B. 1981. Pottery and History. In Anderson and Anderson (eds) 1981, 517–535.

Evans, Jeremy 1988. All Yorkshire is Divided into Three Parts; Social Aspects of Later Roman Pottery Distribution in Yorkshire. in J. Price and P. R. Wilson (eds), *Recent Research in Roman Yorkshire*, 323–337. Oxford: British Archaeological Reports (British Series 193).

Evans, Jeremy 1989. Crambeck; the Development of a Major Northern Pottery Industry. In P. R. Wilson (ed.), *Crambeck Roman Pottery Industry*, 43–90. Leeds.

Fulford, Michael G. 1975. *New Forest Roman Pottery*. Oxford: British Archaeological Reports (British Series 17).

Fulford Michael G. and Ian R. Hodder 1974. A Regression Analysis of Some Late Romano-British Fine Pottery: a Case Study. *Oxonesia* 39:26–33.

Fulford Michael G. and Karen Huddlestone 1991. The Current State of Romano-British Pottery Studies. London: English Heritage (Occasional Paper no 1).

Gillam, John P., 1970. *Types of Roman Coarse Pottery Found in Northern Britain*. Newcastle.

Gillam, John P., 1981. Roman Pottery and the Economy. In Anderson and Anderson (eds) 1981, 9–24.

Going, Christopher J., 1992. Economic 'Long Waves' in the Roman Period: a Reconnaissance of the Romano-British Ceramic Evidence. *Oxford Journal of Archaeology* 11 (1):93–117.

Greene, Kevin 1992. Review of Fulford and Huddlestone 1991. *Britannia* 23: 362–365.

Griffiths, Karen E. 1989. The Marketing of Roman pottery in Second Century Northamptonshire and the Milton Keynes Area. *Journal of Roman Pottery Studies* 2:67–76.

Jones A. H. M. 1974. *The Roman Economy*. Oxford.

Miller, Daniel 1985. *Artifacts as Categories*. Cambridge.

Millett, Martin 1990. *The Romanisation of Britain*. Cambridge: Cambridge University Press.

Monaghan, Jason 1987. *Upchurch and Thameside Roman Pottery*. Oxford: British Archaeological Reports (British Series 173).

Monaghan, Jason 1993. *The Archaeology of York*, vol. 16/7, *Roman Pottery from the Legionary Fortress*. London.

Monaghan, Jason in prep. The Archaeology of York, vol. 16, The Roman Pottery of York.

Orton, Clive R. and P. A. Tyers 1992. Counting Broken Objects: the Statistics of Ceramic Assemblages. *Proceedings of the British Academy* 77:163–184.

Perrin, J. Rob, 1981. *The Archaeology of York*, vol. 16/2, *Roman Pottery from the Colonia: Skeldergate and Bishophill*. London.

Pollard, Richard 1983. The Pottery. In P. D. Catherall 1983, A Romano-British Pottery Manufacturing Site at Oakleigh Farm, Higham, Kent. *Britannia* 14:103–142.

Reece, Richard 1988. *My Roman Britain*. Cirencester.

Salway, Peter 1981. *Roman Britain*. Oxford: Oxford University Press.

Swan, Vivien G. 1994. Legio VI and Its Men: African Legionaries in Britain. *Journal of Roman Pottery Studies* 5:1–34.

Webster, Graham 1964. *Romano-British Coarse Pottery – a Students Guide*. London: Council for British Archaeology (Research Report 6).

Young, Christopher J. 1977. *The Roman Pottery Industry of the Oxford Region*. Oxford: British Archaeological Reports (British Series 43).

Young, Christopher J. 1980. *Guidelines for the Processing and Publication of Roman Pottery from Excavations*. London: Department of the Environment (Occasional paper no. 4).

13

THEORY, PRACTICE, AND RESEARCH IN AN URBAN UNIT: A PERSONAL PERSPECTIVE

Michael J. Jones

What I offer here is no theoretical essay, rather a comment from the perspective of an urban unit on ways in which we might reconcile theory with practice, and historical approaches with theoretical. There are other, related divergences in the profession which are also causing concern (cf. Cunliffe 1990, on the widening gap between practitioners and academics). I shall have cause to consider two principal issues – the value of theory to the research work of a 'rescue unit', and the apparently wide discrepancy between established Roman (and classical) approaches and those involving explicit theory.

It is now respectable to be explicit too about our different subjective standpoints. I speak partly as a unit director who, although largely concerned on a day to day basis with practical matters, is acutely aware of the need to ensure good research value in what we do; but also someone who, although trained initially as a classicist, has always been attracted by theoretical approaches. I am not the only person in this or other fields who recognises both the faults and the value of the newer ideas (Graff 1992). Being on a generational as well as a professional cusp, I suppose I just about belong to the (then) younger generation of Romano-British archaeologists identified in his quasi-sociological paper by Rick Jones (1987a), certainly to what Jeffrey May (1991) has termed the 'somewhat anarchic generation' impressed by the ideas ferment of the late 1960s. Managing a unit through several different funding eras certainly enhances the ageing process – no wonder so few original directors are in post. But like many of the older generation, I had a classical education, on which little or no impact was made by the radical ideas of social scientists, before moving on to Roman archaeology.

As I made this change, archaeology too was visibly changing in Britain: some geographical models were being borrowed (e.g. Johnston 1984), but the development was most notably inspired by David Clarke's *Analytical Archaeology* (1969). In this period of burgeoning theoretical ideas, a vintage crop of Cambridge 'Arch. and Anth.' graduates (Daniel 1986: 201), had found university posts and helped to develop several Single Honours Archaeology schools. Their graduates and scions in turn have constituted a whole army of recruits to the cause (see Champion 1992 for an analysis of the intellectual history of this development).

These Single Honours Archaeology students, while acquiring valuable knowledge and skills, were mostly spared the pain, not to mention the discipline, of rigorous study of the classical languages, where every letter counts. Not that they lacked for discipline, but it was a more balanced training. In contrast, the pedantry of the classicist can encourage dismissal of brilliant new hypotheses if one or two details are inaccurate. Besides, for many classical students, theorising was hardly encouraged.

Many recruits still enter archaeology through other routes. As a result, the archaeology profession, now numbering several thousand in Britain, contains a wide spectrum of individuals with various strengths and weaknesses. With some notable exceptions, classicists and social theorists are as alike as chalk and cheese. Anthony Snodgrass, who has, like Colin Renfrew, been writing eloquently on the application of theoretical approaches to classical archaeology for a decade (e.g., 1985) has put his finger on part of the problem (1987: 10–11): classical scholars tend to be the sort of people who, like pure scientists, seek a 'right answer': the so-called 'convergent' mind. Yet much of classical archaeology was formerly confined to art-history, and there was plenty of scope for theory here (e.g. Carpenter 1960; Hutchinson 1962 on visual perception in Minoan Crete, and recent ideas on iconography; see also Finley 1985: 18–19). Moreover, its long history as a discipline means that its practitioners are not easily impressed by new ideas and this has accordingly enabled it to examine and subsequently jettison certain theories (Boardman 1989; Dyson 1989), while embracing numeracy, taxonomy, and some social theory (e.g. Morris 1992; Alcock 1993).

Two other factors may, however, make it less penetrable by the uninitiated: the need to undertake detailed, often repetitively tedious (and these days quite unpopular), tasks in order to grasp the subject matter, and the fact that it is undertaken on an international (though particularly European) scale so that new hypotheses require international recognition to be fully accepted. I return to the further implication of the first point later. The significance of the second is that approaches to the classical world are, in several other countries, even more traditional than the British (see Todd 1992), although there are signs of change here too. The reasons are various (see Hodder (ed.) 1992; Harke 1992; Cleuziou et al. 1992), though perhaps more easy to understand in Germany than in France. For all the impressive array of France's '*philosophes*', and the mark left by the historical tradition of Bloch and Braudel, the value of applying social theory seems to be largely dismissed by the leading urban archaeologists.

Some comment is appropriate on historical evidence and current historical approaches. The comparatively generous provision of historical documentation – e.g. for the early medieval period – may have influenced French approaches, but we know of the limitations of documentary evidence. Yet ancient history itself has moved a long way from its former concern with political events seen from the point of view of the prevailing elite. A commonly stated view of the fascination of the Roman period, and particularly Roman Britain, was the interplay between the historical and archaeological sources (e.g. Hartley 1966), also recognising the tendency of hypotheses to become 'facts' or 'factoids' (Millett 1990: preface). We are no longer so content to serve as history's handmaiden (e.g. Reece 1993). Snodgrass, for one (1987: 47–51), has identified the often irreconcilable nature of the two types of evidence for what happened in Roman Britain as well as in Ancient Greece (see also Branigan 1989). Medieval archaeology meanwhile has been undergoing similar upheavals (Champion 1992: 146–47 for a recent summary; Rahtz 1981), but its value for understanding settlement layout and social and economic life is increasingly appreciated by historians.

To sum up so far, there are great discrepancies between classical and theoretical approaches, but there are clear signs that some earlier notions are being abandoned and ideas of proven value are being applied.

My own experience of postgraduate research convinced me of both the value and the limitations of a theoretical framework. In 1970 no-one, as far as I was aware, had attempted to collate all the evidence for Roman fortifications into an 'assemblage of (structural) artefacts', to study them quantitatively and draw inferences and patterns using scatter diagrams. When the work was published (Jones 1975), its audience was more concerned with its value as a compendium of the evidence than the type of approach; Roman forts were not, in any case, an area of study to which the leading (Cambridge) theoreticians were applying their minds. Some established scholars also felt that it lacked, as I was only too aware, an insight into the mind of the Roman military command, and I was encouraged to study important campaigns up to fairly recent times; was this also theory? The warmest reception to the methodological approach came in fact from George Jobey, a prehistorian. Research in this field has continued apace, with radical shifts taking place in perceptions of both the contribution of the patricians to the Roman effort – e.g. the debunking of Agricola (Hanson 1987) – and a greater appreciation of the Roman-native relationship (e.g. Breeze 1982; Rick Jones' current project at Newstead). Considerable advances in understanding have of course been achieved by large-scale excavations of complete forts and other research projects, but few 'big ideas' have come along: one of them being Edward Luttwak's stimulating thoughts on 'Grand Strategy' (1976). Like most big ideas, it represented a leap forward and a great intellectual stimulus, but also contained much which is no longer accepted (Hanson 1989).

There is another significant influence on the direction of postgraduate research, then and subsequently: the views of one's supervisors and patrons and the need to rely on a limited number of influential persons for endorsement. I am not saying that I personally was constrained in what I felt able to achieve, but it is true that at that stage we all need one or two sympathetic champions if we are to find a job (as we do subsequently when we apply for research grants). One can only go so far from the well-worn path of one's patrons at this early stage: later, there is more freedom. This must once have been the case too for the current elite of Romano-British studies, a generation strongly influenced by the genius of Eric Birley and Ian Richmond, and not such a homogeneous bunch as might be suspected from outside (cf. Scott 1990, on the tendency for traditionalists to regard theoreticians as all in the same boat; Bradley 1990). Younger academics will probably accept that scholarship in terms of familiarity with the historical sources and basic dating materials was of a higher order than is apparent now, but of course the exponential increase in data has led to increasing specialism. With the spread of chairs in archaeology Britain became gradually covered with as many different scholars and schools as Iron Age tribes, and, not surprisingly, some of them displayed (friendly) rivalries and expected loyalty from those they considered to be their clients. A contemporary of that generation, Philip Rahtz, has frankly admitted that one of the factors that so attracted him to archaeology was the reflected glory of exciting discoveries, in the tradition of past excavators (1985: 18). With the present emphasis on preservation, the 'kudos game' has largely shifted to the new theoreticians displaying their latest wares at TAG Conferences.

Before I had time to establish my personal position in the national research scene, and to join my peer academic group, I left it largely behind, or more accurately I was myself left behind, when I moved into rescue archaeology at Lincoln in the frenetic days of the early 1970s. With considerable energy, but inadequate resources and moderate (but improving) technical standards, much was recorded before destruction. We were, I suppose, guilty of what has been called the 'positivist fallacy' (Snodgrass 1987: 62) – assuming that what is observable is what is important and can indicate the principal historical features of the site. Our research framework, as in much urban archaeology in Britain and abroad, was guided largely by Martin Biddle's work at Winchester as much as any period-specific problems. Even this approach was too 'modern' for some scholars: e.g. F. H. Thompson (1975: 253) refers to the 'nebulous concept' of urban archaeology. Much that emerged in the 1970s and 1980s is still being digested, as it is analysed and subjected to the latest theories of, say, site formation processes, or quantititave finds analysis.

In the meantime the insecurity of the unit's existence meant that our chief priority at times has been survival, to preserve an organisation with local expertise in the city – a model that is generally accepted as being in the best interests of urban archaeology (Galinie, forthcoming). We appear to have come through the worst, but more than ever have to keep on our toes: a Unit needs political, professional and academic credibility. Techniques have to be continually reviewed and improved where possible, and here the Units have to some extent taken the initiative (e.g. in recording and analysing stratigraphy). Management of projects takes up an increasing amount of time, and theories are constantly changing. We have had to sharpen our image with the developer, the planner, and the public, produce reports appropriate to our markets, and generally be accepted as a 'good thing': educational displays help here if they hit the right note, and of course are an investment for the future in creating a favourable climate for archaeological research.

We suffer in archaeology from what one might term the 'remarkable precedent syndrome': if one Professor in the south of England can get his excavation reports published within three years or if an organisation in the north makes profits out of a tourist scheme, those who hold the purse strings assume that we can all follow suit. Perhaps the greatest challenge to the modern unit is maintaining our greatest resource, a substantial group of energetic professionals who have acquired both technical and local expertise – and the latter takes some while to develop. Naturally most staff are, sooner or later, concerned about job security and so there is a need to ensure a smooth workflow, an art in itself. There is some alarm in the profession that, while it is not difficult to persuade students to undertake small dissertations on various types of material, post-graduate research tends to be directed largely to 'theoretically exciting' problems, while we may soon suffer from a depletion of resources in terms of, say, pottery experts (see also Monaghan, above), and find it difficult to get anyone to do a thesis on a body of historical evidence. Fortunately, some of these problems have been recognised, but action is needed soon (Fulford and Huddleston 1991, reviewed by Greene 1992). I have been surprised how few universities have followed the example of Leicester in establishing courses in post-excavation studies.

Whatever the obstacles, it is in our interest not only to produce publications, but to ensure that our reports are written in an awareness of current research problems, and further to devise new projects which are of solid research value. There may be some new large-scale field projects in the future, but in the context of the preservation ethic, and in a recession, these could be few and far between. At least there are now signs that the conservation role which archaeology is playing in society is not considered to be sufficient without a modicum of research. The planning system can be used to carry out research to aid decision-making, but on a limited scale. In preparing reports, therefore, we must take account of the fact that we may not be able to increase substantially either our database or our knowledge of particular sites and problems within the foreseeable future. Yet there is a great deal of data to hand which can be manipulated more easily than ever before thanks to computers.

For many years, I have struggled to keep pace with the output of work on Roman and later towns. What those of us in the Units need to know is: how can results from our sites illuminate problem areas or test current ideas, for instance, in Lincoln on Roman legionary fortresses and towns. Closer links with universities are one way of keeping in touch. The Roman Society provided some advice several years ago (Wacher (ed.), 1985), and some of its ideas were incorporated into a wider survey of urban archaeology produced by the Council for British Archaeology (Jones and Wacher, 1987). The CBA's Urban Research Committee continues to offer useful support with its study of themes such as victualling and innovation. Among the Roman Society's recommendations for future work, several priorities were of direct application to Lincoln; the fortress plan, any site with well-preserved deposits in a major Roman town, complete examples of domestic and industrial dwellings, suburbs and the urban fringes, the territorium, harbours and waterfronts, and cemeteries, especially those of the later Roman/early Christian period. There is obviously a great deal still worth investigating according to the collective wisdom of the Romano-British 'establishment' (see also Todd 1989). The significance of transitional phases – e.g., the late Roman and early Saxon periods – was recognised and was subsequently prominent in English Heritage's research framework 'Exploring Our Past' (1991). Here, the Roman period did not otherwise feature strongly except as an element in diachronic approaches to larger problems, such as 'towns' and 'landscapes'. Justifiably perhaps, greater emphasis was placed on the native perspective.

It is of course quite appropriate for the archaeological study of the town to follow a multi-period approach: this is also the case in France, where 'la ville' forms research project number one for 'historic' archaeology (hence 'programme H1': Min. Culture 1990). But there is also scope in the French scheme for other major themes, on aspects such as cemeteries, mining and metallurgy, communications, etc., as well as more specific problems such as aspects of 'protohistoric' settlements and their populations, and minor urban and rural settlements, through to some site specific projects. Some of the larger field programmes involve several teams working on different aspects of the same *projet collectif de recherche* (e.g. Guyon (ed.) 1991), whose endeavour and direction are co-ordinated by regular meetings and project reviews. I hope that we can observe such initiatives and learn something from them; in many cases it appears that they do not take place in an awareness of the sort of research framework which many British theoreticans would advocate. It is at the same time true that each country has younger groups of scholars who are getting to grips with the changing theoretical approaches seen in Britain (e.g. Hodder (ed.) 1992). The development of theory during the 1970s largely passed the Units by, no doubt partly because they were so preoccupied with site work, with developing new practical applications and with improving and refining recording systems. Moreover, the difficult language of theory and its apparent lack of application to their problems meant that the effort to grasp its significance did not seem worthwhile. Worse was to follow: new theoretical approaches, new theories, and new techniques, many of them borrowed from other disciplines which were already casting them off, seemed to follow each other even more quickly. Of course, some of them left an obvious mark: e.g. spatial analysis, explicit sampling strategies, environmental context. Others, like ideas on social power (Mann 1976) or centre-periphery, would be the talk of one TAG Conference and unmentioned at the next. It was not too obvious to the uninitiated that these ideas were in fact finding their way into the literature but publication of appropriate papers did usually follow (for the application of centre-periphery relationships, see for instance Rowlands and Larsen 1987; Cunliffe 1988; Champion (ed.) 1989; Parker Pearson 1989; Millett 1990).

Now I know that a year is a long time in archaeological theory but units have only a number of specialists, and for those of us trying to make the best use of our time, the multiple whammy of theory after theory with no simple guide to their value (cf. Hodder 1986; Renfrew and Bahn 1991: 426–34) was quite bewildering. From a student perspective, a year *is* a long time, and the excitement of stimulating ideas obviously found a ready market here. A theoretically aware generation has now found its way into the units, and is carrying out good work. But, as I said above, some of our needs are for skilled practitioners in more tedious, practical tasks: perhaps they need a question to start with? It might also be said, perhaps uncharitably, that some younger academics enjoy and benefit professionally from the kudos of being the first to espouse and propagate a new theoretical application. Even academics who have been more open to new ideas are expressing concern that there is too much theory and not enough practice (e.g. Bintliff 1991, re post-modernism at TAG; Snodgrass 1987: 9, on the need to demonstrate that theories work in practice). At least there is some recognition that theories need to be applied to the Roman period with care. Moreover, the theoretical scene is constantly in flux, a fact which gives traditionalists an excuse not to take it seriously and decision-makers 'a pretext' to decry advice from academics. John Barrett has recognised this and has made a plea for a general agreement on the aims of archaeological research (1989). Competition may be healthy within the subject but a unified standpoint is at times necessary when the value and continuation of research is under attack.

Our needs in the units are for regular and clear communication of what is important, what we should be looking for, how we should be analysing our abundant evidence, and of course several approaches are valid. We need to know how to use the archaeological data to the best effect. I like to think that the forerunner of these TRAC occasions was the volume on *Recent Trends* drafted under Rick Jones' editorship and published in 1991, but largely written in 1986 (R. F. J. Jones 1991). Like much of that volume's contents, my own contribution set out some sort of agenda and although it made a gesture in the direction of theoretical approaches, was not written from a theoretically-informed position (M. J. Jones 1991). It is interesting to note that English Heritage is confronting the problem of the viable sample (Startin 1993), one aspect I did consider, and a thorny problem indeed.

So what should we in places like Lincoln be doing with our evidence? We have some help from historians, although not all of them are yet convinced of the value of archaeological evidence. David Peacock's 1982 study of pottery was a notable exception in impressing ancient historians with the contribution which archaeology can make. No doubt this partly reflects the fact that historians, belonging to a more established discipline, tend not to need to grasp on to theory as much as the new, insecure discipline of archaeology seeking to establish itself in its own right. Yet historical approaches have moved on considerably in recent years. Moses Finley (1985: 18–23; 59–66) discussed the relationship between history and archaeology, and argued that the need is not more exhaustive monographs on individual cities, however scholarly. More important to Finley, who accepted the value of models, would be to establish how the economic system worked to support such a large settlement (see Lazreg and Mattingly 1992 for a good example). Finley's successors have carried the debate further, but no consensus exists (Garnsey et al. 1983; cf. Wallace-Hadrill 1991; Eagles 1990). It is certainly clear that we need to study the urban-rural relationship, which includes studies of environmental samples such as animal bones linked to survey of the hinterland (see Millett 1991 for a recent account of one survey). A variety of relationships is to be expected: as Philippe Leveau, a tireless French fieldworker, has written, towns are not the only element of Romanisation, nor are they synonymous with civilisation, merely a sign of a certain form of it; there are several different types of urban systems, several different types of countryside (Leveau quoted by Vallet 1991: 77). Further help is provided by books like that produced by Dominic Perring on *Roman London* (1991), combining the latest archaeological data with recent theoretical ideas, although for many problems it presents only one of several possible interpretations (e.g., cf. Williams 1990). There is pressure to produce cosy,simple histories, for the local and popular markets; we know that the reality was both more complex and uncertain, and that life for most was always fairly wretched, exploitation rife (e.g. Walsh 1992: introduction).

How then are we reconciling these approaches in Lincoln? Work is advanced on a major publication project, with substantial funding from English Heritage, on those sites excavated before 1988. The academic framework and objectives of this project were largely devised by our then inspector, Mike Parker Pearson, now a lecturer in archaeological theory at Sheffield University, in conjunction with my colleague, Alan Vince, who manages the project. Not surprisingly they take due note of the research framework recently published by English Heritage (1991). Progress on the project is being monitored for English Heritage by Tim Williams, who is known and respected by our team for his helpful and knowledgeable support: he too has had much experience of analysing urban stratigraphy and finds, and his researches into Roman London (e.g. 1990) are worthy of inclusion in this volume.

I want to summarise the themes of the research (Vince (ed.) 1991), which of course covers the post-Roman periods too. The analysis of site and finds data can take place more easily because the data has now been computerised, on a multi-user system. Even with generous support, we have had to be selective, to confine finds reports to those which are of patent value, and to limit our academic objectives to three principal themes, which cover questions to which out present data can be applied. They are:

1. The extent of settlement in Lincoln and its suburbs through time and the development of major foci. Settlement is plotted using the pottery databases to chart the incidence of diagnostic types, supported by a synthesis of the stratigraphic evidence and non-ceramic artefacts. Major foci shifted through time, but they included the principal routes and public buildings. Some attempt is also being made to estimate the changing population level through time (see Marsden and West 1992), and social differentiation in relation to material culture.

2. The study of spatial patterning within the town and its suburbs: was there socio-economic zonation? Evidence for commercial activity will obviously be examined here (see Redman 1986 for a good analysis of this theme at Qsar-Es Seghir).

3. Lincoln's hinterland, its trading contacts and their effect on and relationship to the fortunes of the town itself. Pottery will again be a major, but not exclusive, source of information. No new fieldwork is planned; rather the information on the hinterland will be gathered from published and archive sources.

In the course of the project, another theme – that of the major social transformations of the transitional phases – will emerge and the results will be set in their appropriate academic context. But we realise that there are further important areas which will still require attention in due course: for instance, organic finds and the local environment, for which excavations by the river in 1987–90 produced the most useful data. More work is desirable in the longer term related to the wider environment, and on tenurial arrangements and social relationships, property boundaries and land division.

That programme as far as we can tell, is both 'theoretically informed' and appropriate to the available data. It does not prevent us from pursuing in more detail related problems. I mention some here which are my particular concern.

One is the plan of the forum – analogues need detailed study – and the implication of its design in terms of cultural influence, linked perhaps also to what it symbolised (Jones and Gilmour 1980). Rick Jones (1987b) and Martin Millett (1990: 72–73) have touched on, but in relation to the tribal capitals rather than the *coloniae*. Where do the influences derive from and through which mechanism (Blagg 1990; Blagg and Millett (eds) 1990)? The original inhabitants of the military colonies, those who oversaw the development of public-works, were predominantly the retired legionaries who had origins in the Mediterranean area – or so it is assumed; is this distinction reflected in architectural styles and what does this tell us about both the clients and the designers? Can we recognise a distinct elite culture in the early coloniae? If so, when does it cease to be distinctive?

Another major area of research is the nature of the late Roman town, and the symbolic and economic implications of its fortifications (Jones 1993; Jones et al. forthcoming). Some work has already been undertaken on the source of building materials for the city's strong defences, which survived as a 'relict feature' to influence subsequent topography (Jones 1980; cf. Greene 1986: 152–54).

I want to end with the last 'live' remnant of *romanitas* in the city. The existence of an early church-like structure in the middle of the forum was established in 1978, dated to no earlier than the late 4th century, and if you believe the radiocarbon dates of nearby burials, possibly gone by the end of the 6th (Jones 1994). Again it can be viewed as a symbol of power. There is no exact parallel for this phenomenon, although the Exeter forum may have contained a similar structure in the sub-Roman period. Nor is there any certainty in the interpretation of the evidence: I have, therefore been examining better-preserved evidence for early churches in Gaul and the Mediterranean provinces as well as in Britain. The research has suggested several alternative interpretations; e.g., was this part of the 'episcopal group'? Study of the continental evidence is helped by the existence – especially in those Catholic countries which boast better urban continuity – of the thriving discipline of 'Christian archaeology' (Duval 1991). Is it an appropriate appraoch (cf. James 1993)?

This fragmentation of various branches of archaeology, in different ways from in Britain (there is also a 'Merovingian archaeology' in France), strikes one when studying mainland Europe. The different disciplines do not necessarily mix. It is a problem from which we too suffer. As theory advances quickly, much Roman archaeology is still firmly rooted in the traditional disciplines. Let us by all means have a healthy and unrestrained theoretical development, but most of all, let us communicate with each other.

POSTSCRIPT AND ACKNOWLEDGEMENTS ————

Since this paper was written and delivered to the publishers, some echoes of its content can be found, set out more eloquently, in the volume *Archaeological Theory: Who Sets the Agenda?* edited by Norman Yoffee and Andrew Sherratt (Cambridge University Press, 1993). The papers by Richard Bradley, Christopher Chippindale and the editors themselves are of most relevance to the substance of the paper above.

Three reviews of Martin Millett's *The Romanization of Britain* which have now appeared form a useful collection. Although all are by the middle generation of scholars, they take some issue with both Millett's general approach and some of his detailed arguments. See M. G. Fulford in *The Archaeological Journal* 148 (1991): 307–09; R. J. A. Wilson in *Journal of Roman Studies* 82 (1992): 290–03; and P. W. M. Freeman in *Journal of Roman Archaeology* 6 (1993): 438–45.

The paper as here presented is a revised version of that read at the conference, with some of the more ephemeral and flippant material deleted. I thank the organisers of the conference for agreeing to include such an eccentric contribution and subsequently to publish it. In its present form I take full reponsibility for any errors and misrepresentations, but need to register my debt to the following, who kindly commented on an earlier draft and who were without exception encouraging in their response: Dr D. G. Coombs, Pamela Graves, Dr R. F. J. Jones, Dr D. J. Mattingly, Dr M. Millett, Dr M. Parker Pearson, and Peter Rush. Much of the research for this paper was undertaken during my tenure of an Honorary Simon Professional Fellowship of the University of Manchester, and I thank Professor G. D. B. Jones and Dr J. P. Wild for their support.

Bibliography

Alcock, Susan 1993. *Graecia Capta: The Landscapes of Roman Greece*. Cambridge: Cambridge University Press.

Barley, Maurice W. (ed.) 1977. *European Towns: Their Archaeology and Early History*. London: Academic Press.

Barrett, John C. 1989. Archaeology in the Age of Uncertainty. Paper given to Theoretical Archaeology Group Conference 1989.

Barrett, John C., Andrew P. Fitzpatrick, and Lesley MacInnes (eds) 1989. *Barbarians and Romans in North-West Europe*. Oxford: British Archaeological Reports (International Series 471).

Bintliff, John 1991. Post-Modernism, Rhetoric and Scholasticism at TAG: the Current State of British Archaeological Theory. *Antiquity* 65:274–278.

Bintliff, John (ed.) 1991. *The 'Annales' School and Archaeology*. Leicester University Press.

Blagg, Thomas F. C. 1990 The Temple at Bath (Aquae Sulis). *Journal of Roman Archaeology* 3:419–430.

Blagg, Thomas F. C. and Martin Millet (eds) 1992. *The Early Roman Empire in the West*. Oxford.

Boardman, John 1989. Classical Archaeology: Whence and Whither? (Review of Snodgrass 1987). *Antiquity* 62:795–797.

Bradley, Richard 1990. Review of Todd (ed.) 1989. *Britannia* 21:393–396.

Branigan, Keith 1989. Review of Snodgrass. *Journal of Hellenistic Studies* 109: 248–249.

Breeze, David J. 1982. *The Northern Frontiers of Roman Britain*. London: Batsford.

Carpenter, Rhys 1960. *Greek Sculpture: a Critical Review*. Chicago and London.

Champion, Timothy (ed.) 1989. *Centre and Periphery: Comparative Studies in Archaeology*. London: Unwin Hyman.

Champion, Timothy 1992. Theoretical Archaeology in Britain. In Hodder (ed.) 1992, 129–160.

Cleuziou, S., Anick Coudart, J.-P. Demoule, and Alain Schnapp 1992. The Use of Theory in French Archaeology. In Hodder (ed.) 1992, 91–128.

Cunliffe, Barry W. 1990. Publishing in the City. *Antiquity* 64:667–671.

Cüppers, Heinz 1990. *Die Römer in Rheinland-Pfalz*. Stuttgart.

Daniel, Glyn 1986. *Some Small Harvest*. London.

Duval, Noël et al. (eds) 1991. *Naissance des Arts Chrétiens*. Paris: Imprimerie Nationale.

Dyson, Stephen 1989. The Relevance for Romanists of Recent Approaches to Archaeology in Greece. *Journal of Roman Archaeology* 2:143–146.

Eagles, Donald 1990. *Roman Corinth*. Chicago.

English Heritage 1991. *Exploring Our Past: Strategies for the Archaeology of England*. London.

Finley, Moses 1985. *Ancient History: Evidence and Models*. London.

Fulford, Michael G. 1992. Will Preservation be the Death of Archaeology? Paper read at IFA Annual Conference, April 1992.

Fulford, Michael G. and Karen Huddleston 1991. *The Current State of Romano-British Pottery Studies*. London: English Heritage.

Galinie, H. forthcoming. British Archaeology: a View from Abroad. Council for British Archaeology (Annual Report, 1992).

Garnsey, Peter, Keith Hopkins, and C. Richard Whittaker 1983. *Trade in the Ancient Economy*. London: Chatto and Windus.

Graff, Gerald 1992. *Beyond the Culture Wars*, New York and London. W W Norton (reviewed by Patrick Wright). *The Guardian*, 1 June 1993.

Greene, Kevin T. 1986. *The Archaeology of the Roman Economy*. London: Batsford.

Greene, Kevin T. 1992. Review of Fulford and Huddleston 1991. *Britannia* 23:362–365.

Guyon, Jean 1991. From Lugdunum to Convenae. *Journal of Roman Archaeology* 4:89–122.

Hanson, William S. 1987. *Agricola and the Conquest of Britain*. London.

Hanson, William S. 1989. The Nature of Roman Frontiers. In Barrett et al. (eds) 1989, 55–63.

Härke, Heinrich 1992 All Quiet on the Western Front? In Hodder (ed.) 1992, 187–222.

Hartley, Brian R. 1966 Some Problems of the Roman Military Occupation of the North of England. *Northern History* 1:7–23.

Hodder, Ian R. 1986. *Reading the Past*. Cambridge: Cambridge University Press.

Hodder, Ian R. (ed.) 1992. *Archaeological Theory in Europe*. London and New York: Routledge.

Hutchinson, R. W. 1962. *Prehistoric Crete*. Harmondsworth: Penguin.

James, Edward 1993. Review of Duval 1992. *Medieval Archaeology* 37: 340–341.

Johnston, Ronald J. 1984. *City and Society: an Outline for Urban Geography*. 2nd edition. London.

Jones, Michael J. 1975. *Roman Fort Defences to AD 117*. Oxford: British Archaeological Reports (British Series 21).

Jones, Michael J. 1991. Lincoln. In R. F. J. Jones 1991 (ed.), 69–74.

Jones, Michael J. 1993. The Latter Days of Roman Lincoln. In Alan G. Vince (ed.), *Pre-Viking Lindsey*, 14–28. Lincoln.

Jones, Michael J. 1994. St Paul in the Bail: Britain in Europe? In K. S. Painter (ed.).

Jones, Michael J. and B. J. J. Gilmour 1980. Lincoln; Principia and Forum: a Preliminary Report. *Britannia* 11:61–72.

Jones, Michael J. and John S. Wacher 1987. The Roman Period. In John

Schofield and R. H. Leech (eds), *Urban Archaeology in Britain*, 27–45. London: Council for British Archaeology (Research Report 61).

Jones, Michael J. et al. forthcoming. *The Defences of the Lower City: Archaeology of Lincoln*, vol. 7.2.

Jones, Richard F. J. 1987a. The Archaeologists of Roman Britain. *Bulletin of the Institute of Archaeology, London* 24:85–97.

Jones, Richard F. J. 1987b. A False Start? The Roman Urbanisation of Western Europe. *World Archaeology* 19:47–57.

Jones, Richard F. J. (ed.) 1991. *Roman Britain: Recent Trends*. Sheffield: J. R. Collis.

Lazreg, M. B. and D. J. L. Mattingly 1992. *Leptiminus (Lamta)), A Roman Port City in Tunisia*, vol. 1. Michigan.

Luttwak, Edward 1976 *The Grand Strategy of the Roman Empire*. Baltimore: Johns Hopkin University.

Mann, Michael 1976. *The Sources of Social Power*, vol. 1. Cambridge: Cambridge University Press.

Marsden, Peter and Barbara West 1992. Population Change in Roman London. *Britannia* 23:133–140.

May, Jeffrey 1991. Tony Gregory: Reflections on a Life. *Current Archaeology* 126:263–267.

Millett, Martin 1990. *The Romanization of Britain*. Cambridge: Cambridge University Press.

Millett, Martin 1991. Roman Towns and Their Territories: an Archaeological Perspective. In J. Rich and A. Wallace-Hadrill (eds) 1991, 169–190.

Ministère de la Culture 1990. *La Recherche Archéologique en France 1985–89*. Paris.

Morris, I. 1992. *Death, Ritual and Social Structure in Classical Antiquity*. Cambridge: Cambridge University Press.

Painter, K. S. (ed.) 1994. *Churches Built in Ancient Times: Early Christian Architecture in the East Mediterranean, Britain and Ireland*. London: Society of Antiquaries (occasional paper).

Parker-Pearson, Michael 1989. Beyond the Pale: Barbarian Social Dynamics in Western Europe. In Barrett et al. (eds) 1989, 198–226.

Peacock, David P. S. 1982. *Pottery in the Roman World: an Ethnoarcheological Approach*. London and New York: Longman.

Perring, Dominic 1991. *Roman London*. London: Seaby.

Rahtz, Philip A. 1981. The New Medieval Archaeology. Inaugural lecture, University of York.

Rahtz, Philip A. 1985. *Invitation to Archaeology*. Oxford: Blackwell (rev. ed. 1991).

Redman, Charles L. 1986. *Qsar-es-Seghir: an Archaeological View of Medieval Life*. New York.

Reece, Richard M. 1993. Theory and Roman Archaeology. In E. Scott (ed.), *Theoretical Roman Archaeology: First Conference Proceedings*, 29–38. Aldershot: Avebury (Worldwide Archaeology Series 4).

Renfrew, A. Colin and Paul Bahn 1991. *Archaeology: Theories, Methods and Practice*. London.

Rich, John and Andrew Wallace Hadrill (eds) 1991. *City and Country in the Ancient World*. London and New York: Routledge.

Rowlands, Michael G., K. Larsen, and Kristian Kristiansen (eds) 1987. *Centre and Periphery in the Ancient World*. Cambridge.

Scott, Eleanor 1990. Review of Todd (ed.) 1989. *Antiquity* 64:953–956.

Snodgrass, Anthony 1985. The New Archaeology and the Classical Archaeologist. *Am. Journal of Archaeology* 89:31–37.

Snodgrass, Anthony 1987. *An Archaeology of Greece: the Present State and Future Scope of a Discipline, (Sather Classical Lectures)*. Berkeley, Los Angeles and London: University of California Press.

Startin, D. William A. 1993. Preservation and the Academically Viable Sample. *Antiquity* 255:421–426.

Thompson, F. Hugh 1979. Reveiw of Barley (ed.) 1977. *Germania* 57:251–256.

Todd, Malcolm (ed.) 1989. Research on Roman Britain 1960–89. London: Roman Society (Britannia Monograph 11).

Todd, Malcolm 1992. Reveiw of Cüppers 1990. *Journal of Roman Studies* 82:289–290.

Vallet, J. P. 1991. The Place and Role of the Annales School in an Approach to the Roman Rural Economy. In J. Bintliff (ed.) 1991, 73–92.

Vince, Alan G. (ed.) 1991. *Lincoln Excavations 1972–87: Analysis and Publication Research Design*. Lincoln: City of Lincoln Archaeology Unit.

Wacher, John S. (ed.) 1987. *Priorities for the Preservation and Excavation of Romano-British Sites*. London: Roman Society.

Wallace Hadrill, Andrew 1991. Elites and Trade in the Roman Town. In Rich and Wallace-Hadrill (eds) 1991, 241–272.

Walsh, Kevin 1992. *The Representation of the Past*. London and New York.

Williams, Tim 1990. The Foundation and Early Development of Roman London: a Social Context. *Antiquity* 64:599–607.

14

WOMEN AND GENDER RELATIONS IN THE ROMAN EMPIRE

Eleanor Scott

INTRODUCTION ————

The paper I delivered at TRAC 92 has been largely reproduced elsewhere (Scott 1993a: 5–22), but I am grateful for the opportunity to expand on and consolidate a particular theme which I have raised previously and all too briefly, namely that women continue to be invisible within Roman archaeology and ancient history. This situation is dependent partly upon an uncritical over reliance on the ancient literary sources with archaeology relegated to the role of 'handmaiden' (i.e. there to support not to challenge). It has also been mooted that classical philologists are not best trained and equipped to interpret the human cultures of antiquity (MacMullen 1990: 25), yet the views, interests and perspectives of philologists often continue to hold sway with many historians and classical archaeologists. This leads us to the most important and intriguing reason for the invisibility of women in Roman studies, which is the lack of explicit use of feminist social theory in Roman archaeology and ancient history.

Recently, I was assured that comments such as those above are simply 'abstractions' which while easy to rant about vaguely are difficult to demonstrate formally, the implication being that my allegations of androcentrism in Roman studies are unfounded. I would like, therefore, to support and illustrate my contentions more specifically, using examples from Romanist mainstream literature, within a framework of feminist critique.

My interest in feminist critique grew rapidly during the period of my doctoral research (Scott 1988) when it became increasingly clear that various authorities' assertions regarding Roman period infant burials seemed to be based on little more than their own bizarre and prurient notions about the alleged universal prevalence of baby-dropping (Cocks 1921: 150; Johnston 1983: 11; Watts 1989: 373). Indeed, these scholars seemed to envisage naughty Romano-Victorian serving wenches stuffing the illegitimate results of concealed pregnancies into sundry nooks and crannies about the house and yard. This in itself reveals one of the attractions of Roman archaeology for many: the undiluted opportunity for the telling of the ripping yarn. Whether the story is actually appropriate to any specific historical and social context under study would appear to be of little importance. This sleek and slack approach, as we will see later, is nowhere more evident than in discussions of women.

FEMINIST SOCIAL THEORY ————————

There is now extensive literature on feminist social and political theory. There is also a rapidly expanding 'backlash' literature, which seeks to persuade women that too much equality, opportunity, feminism etc. is bad for them, or contrary to 'nature' (Faludi 1992). Thus we see the appearance of tracts from the Institute of Economic Affairs asserting that 'women . . . are genetically predisposed to have other priorities than paid work' (Quest 1992: 2) and further that 'changing nappies does, in fact, have a significant genetic component' (Levin 1992: 20). A significant part of this New Right's argument is underpinned by an idea of 'traditional values' and 'historic precedent', and history and historical archaeology have been much misused within the anti-feminist domain. It is imperative that we begin to write real women into our archaeological narratives and examine the cultural constructions of gender within various historical contexts. I have outlined the political reasons for doing so, but there are also mainstream intellectual reasons, as Ruth Tringham recently noted in a description of her own 'conversion' (Tringham 1991: 94):

> And then it dawned on me . . . until, as an archaeologist, you can learn to give imagined societies faces, you cannot envisage gender. Or, in somebody else's terms (Conkey's?) you cannot engender prehistory. And until you can engender prehistory, you cannot *think* of your prehistoric constructions as really human entities with a social, political, ideological, and economic life. Ahaaaa!

(N.b. It is quite alright to substitute 'prehistory' with 'history' or even 'Roman history'; the world will not come to an end).

Making Women Invisible in Social Analyses: 'Tricks of the Trade'

It is commonly held by feminists, and with good reason, that historical, social and political narratives and theory were, and for the most part still are, written by men, for men and about men (Thiele 1992: 26). This has been dubbed 'male-stream theory' (O'Brien 1981: 5). A number of feminist scholars have investigated women's disappearance from male-stream scholarship by identifying the forms their invisibility takes in androcentric sociology. The three main forms of invisibility identified are *exclusion, pseudo-inclusion* and *alienation* (March 1982; Thiele 1992: 26–28). These forms of invisibility are not mutually exclusive, but rather tend to be used in combination; and they can clearly be identified in mainstream Romanist scholarship.

Exclusion

Invisibility of this form is brought about by women being completely ignored or neglected because the subjects of such theories are explicitly male or male-dominated institutions and activities. Women are excluded by default. They are invisible because they are disregarded. The general narratives and theories set priorities in subject matter and data which focus attention on social processes and activities in which women were only marginally involved, if at all (Thiele 1992: 26). Thus, many volumes sporting the titles *The Roman Empire* or *The Roman World* are in fact accounts of the Roman army, its imperial politics and Roman provincial administration. This is clear from the contents pages of many volumes, two which are reproduced here:

The Roman Empire by Professor Colin Wells (1984):

I   The new order
II   The sources
III   The work of Augustus
IV   Italy under Augustus: the social and political climate
V   The consolidation of the Principate
VI   The army and the provinces in the first century AD
VII   'Emperors made elsewhere than at Rome': Galba to Trajan
VIII The state of Italy from Petronius to Pliny
IX   The orderly government of the Empire: Hadrian to Marcus Aurelius
X   'The immeasurable majesty of the Roman peace'
XI   An age of transition: from Commodus to Maximinius the Thracian

Even the most promising sounding chapters disappoint with their exclusionary language. Thus, in 'Italy under Augustus: the social and intellectual climate' we are told (Wells 1984: 87):

> A motif of Augustan propaganda was the restoration of stability. Just as his legal powers were based on Republican precedent, just as he revived obsolete or obsolescent religious ceremonial, just as those who shared his views, like Livy and Horace, looked back to the good old days of uncorrupted simplicity, so too Augustan art and architecture followed traditional models.

Not one word does he write about women, at whom, as we shall see below, the Emperor Augustus's 'traditional values' campaign was largely directed.

The Roman Empire by Professor Chester G. Starr (1984):

I	Augustus
II	The imperial succession
III	The Roman aristocracy
IV	Governing the Empire
V	The cities of the Empire
VI	Army, roads and frontiers
VII	The first test (AD 211–330)
VIII	The final test (AD 330–476)

Starr too uses exclusionary language, such as in the passage subheaded 'Cultural and religious changes' (Starr 1982: 136):

> If there was no inner sustenance to be gained from the models of the past, then it was time to carve a new approach to the inner nature of mankind which had once animated these models; this was the achievement of the third and fourth centuries after Christ, one of the great turning points of Western civilization. To define succinctly – and so with dangerous precision – the character of these new ideas, man came to visualize himself as an entity independent of state and community. He was sharply distinguished from all other human beings and was also clearly set off from the physical world about him, unlike in the pantheistic view of the classical world. Nonetheless he had vital links to two outside forces: the divine power above, and his fellow men; for he now advanced to the capability of intimate, truly spiritual union with his brothers. So he might work for common aims in a group without sacrificing his individuality, and while separated from the physical world he was certain that it too was divinely governed.

Starr's passage demonstrates a far less subtle form of exclusion, in which women are, for no given reason, simply dropped from the discourse. Thiele notes the work of Hobbes as a prime example, for he presents a Commonwealth entirely inhabited by men. Comparisons with Starr's *Roman Empire* are perhaps inevitable. Thiele stresses that the exclusion of women is an active process rather than a result of passive neglect (Thiele 1992: 27):

> It is not a simple case of lapsed memory: these theorists don't just forget to talk about women; rather, women are structurally excluded from the realm of discourse or, for the sake of theoretical preoccupations and coherency, they are deliberately dropped.

Pseudo-Inclusion

Pseudo-inclusion differs from exclusion in that the theory appears to take women into account but then marginalises them. Women become defined as a 'special case', as anomalies, exceptions to the rule which can be noted and then forgotten about. What is normative is male (ibid.: 27-28).

This is particularly true of the treatment of burial data by many Roman archaeologists. Imbalances in the sex ratios in cemeteries tend to be 'explained away' or dismissed with imaginative stories, and sociological discussion is absent. Sometimes skeletons are even sexed on the most dubious of grounds. Thus Frere viewed the Hambleden infant burials (unsexed) as evidence of 'the exposed unwanted female offspring of a slave-run establishment' (1967: 266-67) with no further discussion. Frere has created an interesting story but in so doing has actually dismissed these burials, and this type of interpretation has become embedded in many secondary sources. When Perring (1991: 121-22) discusses the cemetery data for Roman London and the surrounding area, he *concludes* with the remark, 'Where are the women?' This remark could have been a useful starting point for discussion, but unfortunately it brings the passage to a close and the burial data is explained away in terms of an incomplete sample, which in effect categorises the female burials as a deviation from the norm. The opportunity for discussion of the profound social implications of the burials is lost.

We can also see pseudo-inclusion in operation in *Who Was Who in the Roman World* (Bowder 1980; reviewed in Scott 1993a: 9-10). In brief, the authors endeavoured 'to include all historical and cultural figures of importance' (Bowder 1980: 9). A sample of the large A-D section reveals that only about 7% of these figures are women, though interestingly a much higher percentage appear in the supplementary index of persons alluded to in the text but 'not important enough to be given their own entry' (ibid.). This statement begs (unanswered) questions about whether this number is a fair, proportionate and useful representation of the available material evidence, how 'importance' has been assessed here, and the relationship of this 'scholarship' to the biases of the ancient sources. There is a real disparity between the lengths of the entries of women and men, irrespective of their renown, and women are frequently dismissed in a few lines. Julia Domna receives only 17 lines, whereas relatively obscure male military figures receive two to three times as much. One repeatedly gains the impression that the editorial line incorporates the unspoken belief in the secondary importance of women to men.

Alienation

This form of invisibility refers to those theories which are 'extensionally male' (Clark and Lange 1979: ix). They include women as subjects, but they do not speak of the parameters of women's lives without distortion. Women's experience is interpreted through male categories because the methodologies and values of the theorists remain androcentric. Despite any commitment they may have to the subject of women, their perspective interferes with their interpretation of women's experience, especially in their selection of those parts of women's lives which are deemed significant (Thiele 1992: 28).

Thus we have Matthews (1988: 357) giving women specific space – a whole page no less – in his chapter on 'Roman life and society' in *The Roman World* (Boardman et al. 1988). He deems as worthy of discussion only three categories of women's lives, the roles of helper, prostitute, and mother/homemaker – Man's helpmeets, whores and madonnas (Scott 1993a: 10–11).

Returning to *Who Was Who in the Roman World*, one can see that the entries of the few women who are included tend to incorporate certain common themes, a core of androcentric mythology about women. They were renowned for their beauty; they were renowned for their chastity or their promiscuity; they were the wives, mothers and daughters of important men; they were the victims or perpetrators of violence; they were very fertile or they were barren; or they were the 'real power behind the throne' (ibid.: 9).

MAINSTREAM ROMAN ARCHAEOLOGICAL WRITING ⸺

The Effects of Reliance on the Ancient Sources

A major part of the appeal of Roman archaeology is widely held to be that the Romans themselves documented their own society. Ancient writers such as Pliny, Cato, Columella, Varro, Juvenal and Martial wrote about Roman culture, and modern archaeologists and ancient historians have made prolific use of this window on the past. The ancient sources are thus cited on many subjects. If we want to know all about women in the Roman empire, we need look no further than Pliny. Garnsey and Saller did not look much further, at any rate, when illustrating the 'Family and the household' chapter of their generally well-received, if not seminal, study, *The Roman Empire: economy, society and culture* (1987). They express the usual token caution about accepting the ancient sources too uncritically, and indeed one would hope so when to illustrate the widespread happy subordination of the Roman wife in marriage they cite an absolute gem from the pen of Pliny (131–32). Pliny, in his forties, had married the teenage Calpurnia, and wrote to his aunt thus (Pliny *Ep.* 4. 19):

> I do not doubt that it will be a source of great joy to you to know that [Calpurnia] has turned out to be worthy of her father, worthy of you and worthy of her grandfather. Her shrewdness and frugality are of the highest order. She loves me – a sign of her purity. To these virtues is added an interest in literature, which she has taken up out of fondness for me. She has, repeatedly reads, and even learns by heart my works. What anxiety she feels when I am about to speak in court! What joy when I have finished! She arranges for messengers to tell her of the approval and applause I win as well as the outcome of the case.

Having cited Pliny's letter, what conclusions might we draw? Does this give us a priceless window on the past? On the contrary, one might be inclined to dismiss it as the rantings of a rather unpleasant, arrogant, defensive, pompous, mean, dishonest man – so surely we can't extrapolate from this about Roman marriages in general? Garnsey and Saller would appear to believe that we can, and their rather unsubtle reading of this passage is presented as evidence for women's behaviour and of the widespread cheerful subordination of wives to their husbands, by their subsequent references to Pliny and Calpurnia's 'companionate marriage' and Calpurnia's role as 'youthful admirer'.

This is an example not so much of deliberate *exclusion* of women from the analysis, but rather of the techniques of *pseudo-inclusion* and *alienation*, where women are mentioned or discussed but are then marginalised, set aside from what the authors perceive as the normative and more important male experience, or they are only discussed in terms of selected categories.

Garnsey and Saller's remarks are perhaps simply naive, but nevertheless they deeply flaw their discussion, for although they accept that Pliny has found in Calpurnia the traditional ideal of an aristocratic wife, they are judging her entirely within the very idealised framework created by the Roman writers like Pliny. They have, in effect, fallen for Pliny's rhetoric. So we are presented not with an analysis of Pliny's idealised world, but rather with a self-conscious and uncomfortable series of anecdotes gleaned from the pens of various male aristocrats which are intended to shed light on the actual lives of women; but their comments are at times astonishingly uncritical. For example, Pliny's remark that Calpurnia took up literature 'out of fondness' for him is used to support the thesis that (1987: 134):

> Though some women displayed literary talent, they were not as a rule educated to the same level as their husbands.

That Calpurnia may have had a motive other than pleasing her husband in taking up literature seems to have eluded our two classical scholars, just as it eluded Pliny.

Ancient Literature as Material Culture

There is no need to be entirely negative about these ancient sources. Certainly inferences can be made, so long as it is understood that dependence on literary sources as 'objective historical text' is inherently problematic because the texts are themselves material culture, and the authors – such as Pliny – were human agents acting within and through social and ideological structures, and whose works must therefore be interpreted through reference to these structures. This is a difficult task because these structures have not yet been identified for the Roman world. The ideological realm is not hot property and indeed is not normally discussed in Roman archaeology, which sees its subject matter very much in terms of 'common sense' or early modern explanations. Romanists like to feel that they really can understand the Romans. Thus we have Professor Donald Dudley (1970: 46) arguing in his book, *Roman Society*, that:

> A recent study of Roman women has compared their status to that
> of women in Victorian England. And in that period, before eman-
> cipation, in the full sense, it was usually her own fault if a woman
> let herself be repressed.

Clearly such a disturbing off-the-peg comparison contributes little to an
archaeology of women and gender relations. Yet the ancient literary passages which have been used to bring about such disgraceful interpretations
can have value, if they are used – as I indicated above – as material text
from their specific historical, cultural and ideological contexts. Of course
we do know from ancient sources some of the basic legal edicts issued in
Rome concerning the status of women regarding marriage and property
ownership. A woman and a man could enter into one of three forms of
marriage, the most popular of which (*usus*) was more easy to dissolve than
the others, and within which the woman could own and inherit property.
Legally a women either passed from the *potestas* or authority of her father
to that of her husband, or remained in the authority of her father after
marriage. She had no political rights (Balsdon 1962: 179–80). It should be
stressed that the laws described here, and in fact the writings of the ancient
authors generally, were issued for the landed Mediterranean classes, and
did not apply to slaves. The general descriptive and judgemental writings in
particular cannot be applied to peasants, particularly those in the far-flung
provinces of the empire such as Britain, if indeed they can be confidently
applied to any real women, anywhere.

What is interesting about the laws and their accompanying social
customs is how they were manipulated, negotiated and renegotiated by
men such as the Emperor Augustus to control the lives of women. It would
be useful if Roman archaeologists and ancient historians would discuss
what all these ancient literary passages, and the social complexities that led
to their production, actually meant in the Roman world in terms of images
and propaganda – in terms of the everyday rhetoric and visual images with
which women would have been confronted. Because the women of the
empire have no direct voice, what we have been hearing up until now has
been a noise which has been distorted first through the politics, minds and
pens of ancient writers and secondly through the politics, minds and pens
of modern historians and archaeologists. The voice is distorted out of all
recognition, not surprisingly after such double editing, such double alienation: women's experience has been interpreted twice over through male
categories because the methodology and the values of the theorists remain

androcentric. Thus to find the women of the Roman empire, we must turn to archaeology and the ideological realm, to images in material culture, and look at female ideals and resistance to those ideals that were in operation.

IDEALS AND IMAGES VERSUS REALITY ————

The Acceptance of Myths

Ideal images of women were carried of course in literature, as we have seen regarding Pliny's ideal wife, and there was plenty more rhetoric and propaganda put out by male writers for the literate classes.

It is interesting to note the types of story which have been selected for recent retelling in general works on the Roman empire. A somewhat disturbing trend appears to be the highlighting of 'suicide pact' narratives, where the wife selflessly precedes the husband in death. The modern authors seem to find this rather heroic of the wives, such as Griffin (1988: 1) on the general marvellousness of the Roman empire:

> The idea of Rome has given the West several distinct myths, each full of resonance. There is the image of . . . generals and consuls . . . . [and] great conquerors . . . . Their wives were women like . . . Arria Paeta, who when the Emperor ordered her husband to commit suicide showed the way by stabbing herself with the words 'Look, it doesn't hurt.'

If we return to Garnsey and Saller, we find them still trying to illustrate the 'companionate marriage' with passages from Pliny, this time with the tale of a wife who precedes her terminally ill husband in jumping off a cliff into Lake Como (1987: 134). They do point out that we never hear of a husband bolstering his wife's courage by joining her in death; but they have nevertheless told the tale to illustrate their concept of the 'companionship ideal' in Roman marriage, without exploring the meanings of these myths further. At the very least these stories raise questions about the ideologies of representation and their correspondence with what women 'really' did (see Pollock 1991: 366).

The Augustan Age of 'Traditional Values'

Other ideal images of women were carried in literature, and it is of interest here to note the poem of Horace, commissioned by the Emperor Augustus, written to accompany a fertility festival which acted as the inauguration of the Brave New World and ushered in a new golden age (Balsdon 1962: 79). One part of Horace's commission referred explicitly to Augustus's recent legislation (trans. ibid.):

> Goddess, produce children and give success to the Senate's decrees about the marriage of women and the marriage laws which aim at increasing the birth-rate.

This was part of a general pro-fertility drive by Augustus, to persuade women to have more babies. This included the dedication of the monumental public altar, the Ara Pacis, one panel of which depicted a goddess-woman with two plump infants, surrounded by the fruits of the earth. The imagery on this panel can be read quite simply. The image of the infant, as I have argued elsewhere (Scott 1992) tends to be presented for mass consumption in its most appealing form when it is being used to encourage women to eschew notions of independence, have more babies, and stay home 'nesting'. The Romans went through a sustained phase of such backlash propaganda under Augustus, and it is notable that one of the most naturalistic and attractive Roman depictions of infants is to be found on the Ara Pacis. The imagery clearly links human fertility with abundance and happiness, and the woman's physical presence, posture and garments are clearly intended to invoke in the viewer many different associations – Pax, Venus, Ceres, Italia, Terra Mater, Tellus – all goddesses (Zanker 1988: 174). The goddess is the good, eternal and ubiquitous mother, and the infants are the future of Rome. This was a quite open pro-fertility programme, and ancient Rome saw a rise of restrictive property laws and penalties for unwed and childless women. The message for women was to tow the line and earn nature's 'rewards', or suffer severe consequences.

What about the illiterate classes? The illiteracy of the masses would not have prevented the prevailing ideology permeating their lives, for the messages of Augustus and other administrations were encapsulated in visual images and in poetry and rhetoric, all of which were carried round the empire. The poetry would have been transmitted primarily by bards, and if one looks at the verse of Horace quoted above in the original Latin one can see that its inherent qualities include a quite beautiful and *memorable* cadence. The fertility propaganda of Horace would have reached everywhere.

> Diva producas subolem patrumque
> prosperes decreta super iugandis
> feminis prolisque novae feraci
> lege marita

Relief sculptures – such as the Ara Pacis – and statues, and *copies* of these sculptures and statues, images of perfect goddesses and Roman imperial women, were highly visible in public places. They were transported all over the empire, into every forum and public space in every town, such as the statue from Ostia in Italy of Sabina as the goddess Ceres, and the statues of the Empress Julia Augusta around the empire. There were wall-paintings and mosaics of goddesses in public and private buildings and baths. There were images of goddesses on the reverse sides of coins in circulation, and there were images of women on the samian pottery which we know was in circulation on even the poorest sites in the empire. The uniformity of the imposed culture throughout the empire meant that every woman and man, regardless of status, would be exposed on a daily basis to these idealised images of women. Rome was, after all, a blueprint for every other city, town and even fort in the whole Roman world.

We now begin to see the sets of contradictions presented to women. There were the official images of women as goddesses, imbued with a power and goodness which ordinary women could never attain, but which they would revere. There were the official role models of the imperial matrons, with their extraordinary complex hairstyles and robes to be painstakingly emulated and consumed, regardless of the provincial woman's status or background. And there was the official reality of women in law and Roman social custom and popular literature, disenfranchised and steered toward subordination through a harsh reward-and-punishment regime. It is perhaps noteworthy that the very complex hairstyles were seen primarily in the early empire, in the first and second centuries AD, and one might even begin to think of a cultural colonisation by Rome of the women of the new provinces.

Altered Images?

Sometimes maverick images break through in later years, especially in the late third and fourth centuries, images which seem to challenge the cultural colonisation of the Romans, such as the Celtic triple goddess representations from Roman Britain, and the woman on the Rudston villa 'Venus mosaic' in Yorkshire, with her hair swinging free and her body unencumbered with the complicated Roman garments of the earlier imperial period. Is she a Celtic goddess? Or a real woman? This isn't as important as the uninhibited image itself. The image, however, received rather dismissive treatment from Professor Ian Richmond who wrote about the Rudston pavements in 1963 (Richmond 1963):

The immediate problems presented by the pavements are . . . those of design and taste. Each pavement is different: the first [the 'Venus mosaic'] is lively with figures; the second [a plain geometric tesselated pavement] has a quiet conventional pattern like a rug . . . . The most satisfying to modern taste is unquestionably the second. But the first is in every way the most remarkable; for we can admire the ambition of the designer, while smiling at the execution of subjects beyond his skill . . . . There is no need to dwell on the badness of this work.

Another image from a similar context, that of a fourth century AD Romano-British villa, has produced evidence for the participation of women in mainstream Christian worship. A group of six figures, both adult women and men, were found painted onto a wall at Lullingstone villa in Kent. Taking this evidence together with that for increased ritual infant burials in this period (Scott 1991), I have often wondered if we are not seeing a positive shift for women in gender relations here after 300 years of cultural colonisation by Rome. If it had not been for Christianity, at first a gender equal cult or religion, the dominant religion of the empire might well have been Mithraism, exclusive to men and beloved of the military. The early Christian church was probably an exciting and fulfilling place for women. But then something went wrong. By the fourth century the male church theologians had become thoroughly infected with the misogynist sentiments of the ancients, particularly Aristotle, who saw women as a corrupting force on earth (Sanders and Stanford 1992: 18). St John Crystotom (AD 347–407) wrote:

The whole of her bodily beauty is nothing less than phlegm, blood, bile, rheum, and the fluid of digested food . . . . If you consider what is stored up behind those lovely eyes, the angle of the nose, the mouth and the cheeks you will agree that the well-proportioned body is merely a whitened sepulchre.

Saunders and Stanford carefully argue that the Church's obsession with virginity, closely coupled with the unholiness of the normal, mature woman, was well under way. They observe that 'Having sex with one of these pieces of Adam's rib, said theologians, was the equivalent of embracing a bag of shit' (ibid.).

THE FEMINIST CHALLENGE ———

It has always been a source of great disappointment to me that archaeology has failed so dismally to challenge or provoke discussion of the social theories which our modern democracies are prepared to accept. I suspect that this is because the past which archaeologists write tends to ape conveniently the present they want to condone. Nowhere is this more clear than in the writing about women, particularly the women of the Roman empire. When one thinks that archaeological narratives still tend to be written by men for men, one might wonder just what storyboard games are being played out in the corridors of learning up and down the land. And the storyboards of course get passed on to the public, to school children in museums and to right-wing think tanks.

These comments are not simply made in passing. There is a pressing need for an archaeology of gender relations. Romanists should not feel exempt from this call just because they have information about 'real' women in the form of texts, epigraphy, sculpture, paintings and small finds. On the contrary, the cultural meanings of this data need to be critically assessed. Further, the information presented for study tends to represent the existence of only a small proportion of women from particular social groups, leaving the vast majority of women historically disenfranchised.

I believe that it is through increased analysis of the images of women and a better understanding of the burial evidence, the social construction of space and all the narratives of material culture in the Roman empire that we will be able to write an archaeology of women and gender relations in this period. This would mean Romanists critically examining their conceptual or interpretive frameworks (Scott 1993a), and I think that it is becoming increasingly clear that this would be no bad thing.

My final comment is addressed to those socialist archaeologists who have informed me that one cannot begin to address adequately the issues of androcentrism and gender within archaeology until we have begun to do so in society in general. I am inclined to argue the opposite, because we should not under estimate the influence of perceptions of the past on our present policy makers (or rather, the perceptions they think they can get away with). The macro- and micro-political ideologies of our western democracies are underpinned by a core of traditional mythologies, dressed up and labelled as history and biology, and it is up to those who have primary access to the knowledge which can dispel these myths to challenge vociferously the current orthodoxies. We have the power to counter the politically compromised ideas of 'history' and 'tradition' which are used to sustain the gender imbalances of our society.

188   E. SCOTT

Bibliography

Balsdon, J. P. V. D. 1962. *Roman Women: Their History and Habits*. London: Bodley Head.

Boardman, J., J. Griffin and O. Murray (eds) 1988. *The Roman World. Oxford History of the Classical World*. Oxford: Oxford University Press.

Bowder, D. (ed.) 1980. *Who Was Who in the Roman World*. Oxford: Phaidon.

Clark, L. M. and L. Lange (eds) 1979. *The Sexism of Social and Political Theory: Women and Reproduction from Plato to Nietzsche*. Toronto: Toronto University Press.

Cocks, A. H. 1921. A Romano-British Homestead in the Hambleden Valley, Bucks. *Archaeologia* 71:141–198.

Dudley, D. 1970. *Roman Society*. London: Pelican.

Faludi, S. 1992. *Backlash: the Undeclared War against Women*. London: Chatto and Windus.

Frere, Sheppard S. 1967. *Britannia*. London: Routledge and Kegan Paul.

Garnsey, Peter and R. Saller 1987. *The Roman Empire: Economy, Society and Culture*. London: Duckworth.

Garwood, Paul, D. Jennings, Robin Skeates, and J. Toms (eds) 1991. *Sacred and Profane*. Oxford: Oxford University Committee for Archaeology (Monograph 32).

Gero, Joan M. and Margaret W. Conkey (eds) 1991. *Engendering Archaeology: Women and Prehistory*. Oxford: Blackwell.

Griffin, J. 1988. Introduction. In J. Boardman et al. (eds) 1988, 1–7.

Johnston, D. E. 1983. *Roman Villas*. 2nd edition. Shire.

Levin, M. 1992. Woman, Work, Biology and Justice. In C. Quest (ed.) 1992, 9–26.

MacMullen, Ramsay 1990. *Changes in the Roman Empire: Essays in the Ordinary*. Princeton: Princeton University Press.

McDowell, L. and R. Pringle (eds) 1992. *Defining Women: Social Institutions and Gender Divisions*. Cambridge: Polity Press (Open University).

March, A. 1982. Female Invisibility in Androcentric Sociological Theory. *Insurgent Sociologist* 11 (2):99–107.

Matthews, J. 1986. Roman Life and Society. In J. Boardman et al. (eds) 1986, 338–360.

O'Brien, M. 1981. *The Politics of Reproduction*. London: Routledge and Kegan Paul.

Perring, Dominic 1991. *Roman London*. London: Seaby.

Pollock, S. 1991. Women in a Men's World: Images of Sumerian Women. In J. M. Gero and M. W. Conkey (eds) 1991, 366–387.

Quest, C. 1992. *Equal Opportunities: a Feminist Fallacy*. London: Institute of Economic Affairs Health and Welfare Unit (Choice in Welfare no. 11).

Richmond, Ian A. 1963. *The Rudston Pavements from Rudston, East Riding*. Hull: Hull Museum (Publication no. 215).

Saunders, K. and P. Stanford 1992. *Catholics and Sex from Purity to Purgatory*. London: Heinemann (for Channel Four).

Scott, Eleanor 1988. Aspects of the Roman Villa as a Form of British Settlement. Unpublished Ph.D. thesis, University of Newcastle upon Tyne, Newcastle upon Tyne.

Scott, Eleanor 1991 Animal and Infant Burials in Romano-British Villas: A Revitalization Movement. In Paul Garwood et al. (eds) 1991, 115–121.

Scott, Eleanor 1992. Images and Contexts of Infants and Infant Burials: Some Thoughts on Some Cross-Cultural Evidence. *Archaeological Reveiw from Cambridge* 11 (1):77–92.

Scott, Eleanor (ed.) 1993. *Theoretical Roman Archaeology: First Conference Proceedings*. Aldershot: Avebury (Worldwide Archaeology Series 4).

Scott, Eleanor 1993a. Writing the Roman Empire. In E. Scott (ed.) 1992, 5–22.

Starr, Chester G. 1982. *The Roman Empire 27 BC to AD 476: a Study in Survival*. Oxford: Oxford University Press.

Thiele, B. 1992. Vanishing Acts in Social and Political Thought: Tricks of the Trade. In L. McDowell and R. Pringle (eds) 1992, 26–35.

Tringham, Ruth E. 1991. Households with Faces: the Challenge of Gender in Prehistoric Architectural Remains. In J. M. Gero and M. W. Conkey (eds) 1991, 93–131.

Wacher, John 1974. *The Towns of Roman Britain*. London: Batsford.

Wacher, John (ed.) 1987. *The Roman World*. 2 vols. London: Routledge.

Watts, D. J. 1989. Infant Burials and Romano-British Christianity. *Archaeological Journal* 146:372–383.

Wells, Colin 1984. *The Roman Empire*. London: Fontana.

Zanker, P. 1988. *The Power of Images in the Age of Augustus*. Ann Arbor: University of Michigan.